WHAT IS A

CONFESSIONAL
CHURCH?

WITH THE 1689 CONFESSION

About the author

Boon-Sing Poh was born in 1954 in Malaysia. Brought up in a pagan background, he was saved by God's grace through faith in Jesus Christ while studying in the United Kingdom. He returned to Malaysia to become a lecturer in a university for six years, founded the first Reformed Baptist Church in the country in 1983, and was imprisoned for his faith from 1987 to 1988 for a period of 325 days. He is the pastor of Damansara Reformed Baptist Church (DRBC) in Kuala Lumpur, a contented husband, a thankful father of four sons, and a happy grandfather. He earned the PhD degree in Electronics Engineering from the University of Liverpool, UK, the Diploma in Religious Study from Cambridge University, UK, and the PhD degree in Theology from North-West University, SA.

WHAT IS A

CONFESSIONAL CHURCH?

WITH THE 1689 CONFESSION

BOON-SING POH

PUBLISHED BY GOOD NEWS ENTERPRISE

WHAT IS A CONFESSIONAL CHURCH? WITH THE 1689
CONFESSION

Copyright ©Boon-Sing Poh, 2021

ISBN: 978-983-9180-59-6

First published: December 2021

Published by:

GOOD NEWS ENTERPRISE, 52 Jalan SS 21/2,
Damansara Utama, 47400 Petaling Jaya, Malaysia.
www.rbcm.net; www.ghmag.net

Printed by:
Kindle Direct Publishing, an Amazon company, United States of
America. Typeset by the author using TeXworks, the memoir class.

Cover picture: The city of London. Courtesy of Yeh-Han Poh.

This book is dedicated to

Earl M. Blackburn,

a brother in arms

in the service of

the Lord Jesus Christ.

Contents

PREFACE

A confessional church holds to one of the historic confessions of faith that arose, either directly or indirectly, from the Reformation of the 16th century. Among the better-known confessions of faith are the Three Forms of Unity (encompassing the Belgic Confession, the Heidelberg Catechism, and the Canons of Dort) held by the Calvinist churches of Continental Europe, the Thirty-nine Articles of the Church of England, the Westminster Confession held by Presbyterian churches, the Savoy Declaration of Faith and Order held by Congregational churches, and the 1689 Baptist Confession held by Reformed Baptist churches. Today, many such churches pay lip-service to their confessions of faith and are, therefore, not truly confessional. The General Baptist churches of earlier years held either to the General Baptist Confession of Faith of 1660 or to the Orthodox Creed of 1679. Today, the General Baptists are largely non-confessional, being satisfied with only a brief Statement of Faith.

Among the growing number of individuals and churches that claim to hold to one, or more, of the historic confessions of faith are those who waver in their commitment to those documents. This book is intended primarily to help those who are attracted to the 1689 Baptist Confession of Faith, or who already claim adherence to it. Brethren in other denominations will find some of the material relevant and helpful. The first chapter gives a brief outline of the characteristics of a Reformed Baptist church. The second chapter sketches the origin of the 1689 Confession. The third chapter argues for the legitimacy of using a confession of faith. The fourth chapter shows the difference between strict subscriptionism and loose subscriptionism and, therefore, the difference between true confessionalism and nominal confessionalism. The fifth chapter shows what are involved in upholding the spirit of 'semper reformanda' while holding firmly to the 1689 Confession. Much of the contents of these chapters have been published elsewhere.

The second part of the book consists of the 1689 Confession in modern English. It is not a paraphrase, but a re-statement of the document, to stay faithful to its contents. This is done not to compete with the versions produced by others but arose from the effort of the present writer in translating the confession of faith into Indonesian. Archaic words are replaced with modern ones, long sentences have been shortened, and the positions of words have been altered for greater clarity. Punctuations have been altered and contents have been separated into paragraphs where deemed necessary.

My dear wife, Goody, has been a constant and supportive companion. Our four sons and their respective families are a great comfort to us. The members of the Damansara Reformed Baptist Church have proved their mettle as they stood with us in the trials and triumphs of gospel ministry. The present writer is alone responsible for the contents of this book.

It is hoped that this book will help a new generation of believers in their walk with God. May all the tribes of the Israel God increase!

Boon-Sing Poh,
Kuala Lumpur, December 2021.

Part I

CONFESSIONALISM

One

WHO ARE THE REFORMED BAPTISTS?

1.1 History

After the time of the apostles, churches continued to multiply everywhere. As the years passed, many churches began to depart from the teachings of the Bible. Superstition and human traditions were propagated as truth. Wars were waged in the name of Christianity. Immorality, idolatry and corruption were rampant in the so-called Christian world. The true Christians were a persecuted minority.

In the 16th century, God brought about a mighty stirring in Europe, causing many people to seek Him and hunger after the truth. This is now called the Reformation. Despite the attempts of the older churches to counter this movement, new churches were founded right through to the 17th century.

In England, the Particular Baptist churches arose in the first half of the 17th century. They were known as *Baptists* because, unlike the other reformed churches, they held to the baptism of believers by immersion. They were known as *Particular* Baptists because, unlike the General Baptists, they held to the doctrine of "particular redemption", i.e. the belief that Christ died specifically for the elect. The Particular Baptist churches grew in number quickly in Britain and America, until they were affected by hyper-Calvinism in the 18th century. Hyper-Calvinism distorts the doctrine of the sovereignty of

3

God by denying that it is right to call upon sinners to repent and believe in Christ.

From the 19th century, all evangelical churches were weakened by the rise of modernism. The Particular Baptists were not spared. Modernism (or liberalism) deny the supernatural and miraculous of the Bible in the name of proud scholarship. A man-centred emphasis settled upon the churches. The prevailing laxity and low view of the authority of Scripture allowed the charismatic movement to spread fast in the 20th century, with its characteristic practices of tongue-speaking, prophesying, healing, dancing, the use of high-powered music, etc.

A revival of interest in reformed theology began in the 1960s, focused at first in Britain and America. It began to spread world-wide, so that today a reformed movement is found in almost every part of the world. The Baptists and the Presbyterians have bene-fited most from this recovery. The older Particular Baptist churches have been revived and newer Reformed Baptist churches have been founded, the two streams merging to form a worldwide Reformed Baptist movement.

1.2   Distinctives

The beliefs of the Reformed Baptists are summarised in the London Baptist Confession of Faith of 1689. In this document, the major doctrines of the Bible are stated clearly and concisely, yet with suffi-cient fullness so as to provide a useful reference manual in this age of shallowness and confusion.

Apart from referring to this document, how may we describe the Reformed Baptists? Reformed Baptists are characterised by the fol-lowing emphases:

The sovereignty of God
God is all-powerful and in absolute control – in creation, history and salvation. God has predestined certain individuals from before the creation of the world to be saved. These are known as "the elect". Every person is born sinful and is unable to do anything good to make God accept him. God calls out the elect from the world by the proclamation of the gospel, and changes their nature by the power

of the Holy Spirit so that they willingly turn to Christ to be saved. Christ died as a sacrifice in the place of the elect, and rose from death to give them eternal life. Salvation is therefore a free gift of God, not gained by human merit, but received by faith in Christ. This understanding of salvation has been called "Calvinism".

The primacy of God's word
Scripture is the sole authority in all matters of faith and practice. Preaching must occupy the central place in the worship service. The Bible is to be preached in an expository manner – giving the correct meaning and applications, and directed to the conscience of the hearers.

The purity of worship
The worship of God must be carried out "in spirit and in truth", i.e. with sincerity and according to God's word. Whatever is commanded must be followed, while anything not commanded must be rejected. This is sometimes called "the regulative principle". Worship is kept God-centred, at the same time that the worshippers maintain a spirit of reverence, joy, warmth and love.

The purity of the church
The local church is central and unique in the purpose of God. Baptised believers voluntarily covenant together as a church to worship and serve God. A high level of commitment is required of the members, but no higher than what is taught in the Bible. Abilities differ from individual to individual, but the Lord only requires that one does what he is able, and no more. Through the exercise of pastoral oversight and church discipline, the membership is kept healthy and pure. No church is perfect in this world, but that does not mean a church should be allowed to lose its spirituality.

A radical discipleship
Reformed Baptists take seriously the truth that they have been bought by the blood of Christ. They belong to God and wish to glorify God by living in accordance to the teaching of Scripture, even at great personal cost to themselves. They are not extremists who love violence, nor fanatics who disrupt public peace. Conscious that they have been reconciled with God, they actively seek to lead others to faith in Christ. They do not claim to be perfect but, in dependence

upon God, attempt to live holy lives.

1.3   Relationship With Others

How do Reformed Baptists differ from other evangelicals?
There are evangelical churches that show great love for the Lord and
have been mightily blessed by Him. Such churches put us to shame
and make us yearn to live for the Lord better. Having said that, it
remains true that there are evangelicals who are weak in precisely
those five areas that the Reformed Baptists are strong. Many evangelicals think that it is enough to have faith in Christ, to pray, and to
attempt to win souls for Christ. They also have a defective view of
the sovereignty of God and a low view of the authority of Scripture.
Quite many have succumbed to charismatic teaching and practice,
and also compromised the truth by joining the ecumenical movement.

**How do Reformed Baptists differ from other reformed Chris-
tians?**
There are reformed Christians who hold to infant baptism, believing
that the children of believers should be treated as church members
and are therefore to be baptised. They baptise by sprinkling instead
of immersion. The baptism of infants leads to a mixed church membership – one consisting of believers and non-believers. Reformed
Baptists are of the view that only believers should make up the membership of the church.

Some churches claim that they are "reformed" when, in fact, they
show no appreciation of the Reformation nor of the truths recovered
at that time. Others hold to some of those truths but proceed no
further. We do not use the word "reformed'" in those ways.

How do Reformed Baptists differ from other Baptists?
Like the other evangelicals, most of the non-reformed Baptists are
either fully-fledged Arminians or they hold to a modified Arminianism. Arminianism teaches that Christ died for every individual in
the world, and man has free-will which must be exercised to "accept
Christ" so as to be saved.

How do the Reformed Baptist Churches relate to other evangelical churches?

We recognise other churches as true churches of Christ when the fundamentals of the faith are upheld by them. The limitations of time, ability and opportunity means that we have to practise selective fellowship with others. Truth determines the degree of closeness that we forge with other churches – the more of truth we agree upon, the closer is our fellowship, and vice versa. Consequently, our closest fellowship is with other Reformed Baptist churches, followed by other reformed churches, and then other evangelical churches.

How do the Reformed Baptist Churches relate to one another?

We have the same beliefs and practices, although there is not a boring uniformity among the churches. Many churches are associated together in a definite way, sharing resources in mutual support, the training of ministers, and church planting. The church members have the opportunity to meet together in annual church camps, conferences, and other combined meetings that are organised regionally from time to time.

What should I do to find out more about the Reformed Baptists?

Attend the weekly meetings of a church nearest you regularly, for a period of time. Talk to the church members and the elders. They will be able to explain to you more, and help you to get the books recommended below.

1.4 Recommended Reading

1 Chantry, W. 1970. Today's Gospel: Authentic or Synthetic? Banner of Truth Trust.

2 Poh, B. S. 2017. Thoroughgoing Reformation, Good News Enterprise.

3 Poh, B. S. 2017. What is a Reformed Baptist Church? Good News Enterprise.

4 Riddle, Jeffery T. 2019. The Doctrines Of Grace: An Introduction to the Five Points of Calvinism. Trumpet Books).

Two

HISTORY OF THE 1689 CONFESSION

The Second London Baptist Confession Of Faith, also known as "the 1689 Confession" in short, has a long and illustrious history, stretching to the Reformation of the 16th century. Here, we provide a sketch of that history and draw up some implications.

2.1   Events Leading To The Reformation

The early disciples of Jesus Christ carried out the Great Commission, "from Jerusalem, and in all Judea and Samaria, and to the end of the earth (Acts 1:8)." John, after exile to the island of Patmos, was based in Ephesus until his death in AD 98. Mark brought the gospel to Egypt, and Thomas to India. Missions and intermittent persecutions kept the early churches pure in membership and doctrine. There are clear statements of adult baptism upon conversion in the early writings, and no mention of infant baptism. Infant baptism was first mentioned by Tertullian only around AD 220. The Episcopal form of church government began to develop after the death of the apostles. Bishops ruled over many churches in geographical regions called 'dioceses' or 'parishes', helped by lower officials. The Roman Catholic Church and the Eastern Orthodox Churches practise this form of church government. The Church of England, and the Methodist and Lutheran denominations, also practise this form of church government.

The Roman emperor Constantine (AD 272-337) professed faith in AD 312 but did not get baptised until he was on his deathbed. (Some scholars question the genuineness of his conversion, wondering if it was a political tool to unite the empire.) He issued the Edict of Milan in AD 313 which commanded official toleration of Christianity and other religions. Heresies of various kinds – notably on the Trinity and the person of Christ – appeared and were dealt with at the various 'ecumenical councils', some of which were chaired by the Roman emperors. Church and state began to be intertwined. The church of Rome, being located at the capital of the empire, began to grow in prominence. The title 'Pope' (meaning Father) was generally used of all bishops by the early third century. Pope Stephen I (254-257) was the first bishop to explicitly claim primacy over all the churches, although opposed by others. Pope Damasus I (366-384) was the first pope to claim primacy based on Matthew 16:16-19.

Medieval Christianity split into the Eastern Orthodox Catholics and the Roman Catholics when Pope Leo III crowned Charlemagne, King of the Franks, as Holy Roman Emperor in 800. The Eastern Emperor and the Byzantine Empire felt slighted after having withstood the Germanic barbarian invasions and upheld the faith for centuries. (The nomadic tribes in Asia were pushing the Germanic tribes westward.) Back of the political-social divide were disputes over papal authority. The East-West Schism was formally sealed in 1054 when the churches each excommunicated the other. The dissenting groups were persecuted by the establishment churches. These groups included the Albigenses, the Paulicians, the Bogomiles, the Waldensians, the Lollards, and the Anabaptists. They largely kept to believer's baptism, although holding to some doctrinal peculiarities as well.

At the eve of the Reformation, the Roman Catholic Church was particularly influential in the West. Governments were under its influence, while immoral priests ignorant of the Scriptures were propagating superstitious ideas and upholding the human traditions of the church. A priest and theologian by the name of Martin Luther (1483-1546) struggled to find peace with God through asceticism. He finally came to peace with God through faith in Christ, whose imputed righteousness alone assured him of acceptance before God. He began to preach the doctrine of 'justification by faith, in Christ, alone'. The sale of indulgences for the dead ('certificates to heaven') by one Johann Tetzel outraged Luther. The many abuses of the Roman Catholic Church drove Luther to nail the 'Ninety-five Theses', a list of questions and propositions for debate, to the door of the Wittenberg Castle Church in Germany. This event, on 31 October 1517, marked the official beginning of the Reformation.

Martin Luther was called to the town of Worm and urged to renounce his teaching, to which he responded, "Unless I am convinced by the testimony of the Scriptures or by clear reason (for I do not trust either in the pope or in councils alone, since it is well known that they have often erred and contradicted themselves), I am bound by the Scriptures I have quoted and my conscience is captive to the Word of God. I cannot and will not recant anything, since it is neither safe nor right to go against conscience. May God help me. Amen." The doctrine of 'sola scriptura' had been boldly proclaimed. It became known as 'the formal principle of the Reformation' upon which rest the other principles.

2.2 The Spread Of Reformed Theology

As the Reformation spread, other notable Reformers were raised up by God, including Philip Melanchthon, Heinrich Bullinger, Martin Bucer, Ulrich Zwingli, and William Farel. Another was John Calvin (1509-1564), who trained as a lawyer in France, and escaped to Switzerland after his conversion in 1533. Upon being challenged by William Farel about his selfish seclusion for academic pursuit, Calvin came to Geneva to preach. By his preaching and writing he developed the system of theology later called Calvinism, which included the doctrine of predestination and the absolute sovereignty of God in the salvation of man from eternal damnation. Calvin spent his final years promoting the Reformation in Geneva and throughout Europe. One of his students, John Knox, brought the Reformation to Scotland.

The Reformation spread to Britain from the late 16th century to the end of the 17th century. A religious reform movement, known as'Puritanism', arose within the Church of England which spilled over to other denominations. The Great Ejection of 1662 caused 2,000 Puritan ministers to join the Nonconformists in the work of reforming the church. The Puritans were well-known for their preaching and pastoral care. Their writings were most influential, even up to today. They became known as 'the second-generation Reformers'.

Although not expressed as a list until later, the five principles of Reformed theology were clearly characteristic of the teaching of the Reformers and the Puritans. The Latin word 'sola' means 'solely' or 'only'. The five 'sola's' are: (i) *sola scriptura,* by Scripture alone; (ii)*sola fide,* by faith alone; (iii) *sola gratia,* by grace alone; (iv) *solus Christus,* through Christ alone; (v) *soli Deo gloria,* glory to God alone. The Reformed church was troubled by the spread of Arminianism from 1610. The Canons of Dort, published in 1619, helped to stabilise the situation, giving rise to 'the Five Points of Calvinism', which is not to be confused with 'the Five Principles of the Reformation'.

The Puritan Age
More needs to be said about the Puritans. The word 'Puritan' seemed to have been used by the many Anabaptists from continental Europe who were settled in London. During the reign of Queen Elizabeth I (1558-1603), there arose a brotherhood of pastors who were followers of the teaching and spirit of the Reformers. They were labelled 'Puritans' as a term of derision. Sadly, the word is used the same way by many today.

In 1568 there were "many congregations of the Anabaptists in London, who called themselves Puritans, or the unspotted lambs of the Lord". They emphasised the central truths of the Christian faith – faithfulness to Scripture, expository preaching, pastoral care, personal holiness, and practical godliness. The word 'Puritan' began to be used to refer to these people who were scrupulous about their way of life. A well-known Puritan, Richard Baxter (1615-1691), recalled his childhood experience in an English village: "We could not on the Lord's Day either read a chapter, or pray, or sing a psalm, or catechise or instruct a servant, for the noise of the piper and tabor, and shouting in the streets continually in our ears, and we were the common scorn of all rabble in the streets, and we were called Puritans, precisionists, hypocrites because we rather chose on the Lord's Day to read the Scriptures rather than what they did." The Arminian-Calvinist controversy resulted in a new meaning of the term. Those ministers in England who subscribed to the doctrines of grace (the

Five Points of Calvinism) were called 'Puritans'.

Relationship between the Church of England and the Roman Catholic Church had been tenuous since King Henry the VIII (r. 1509-1547). In the reign of Queen Elizabeth I, the Acts of Supremacy and Uniformity were passed in 1559. The Act of Supremacy made her the Supreme Governor of the Church of England, which officially became independent from the Roman Catholic Church. The Act of Uniformity required all to accept the Book of Common Prayer and the way of worship stipulated in it. The ministers had to wear the surplice (a loose white outer garment), make the sign of the cross during prayer, and kneel during communion. These were opposed by the Puritans. This situation continued through the reign of James I (1603-1625), during which the Authorised King James Version of the Bible was translated. Delegates were sent to the Synod of Dort in the Netherlands, which deliberated over the Calvinist-Arminian controversy.

The reign of Charles I (r. 1625-1649) was tumultuous. Charles I ruled without Parliament from 1629 to 1640. From 1640, Parliament met again. Civil war broke out in 1642 between those who supported royalty and those who were on the side of Parliament. The Scottish Parliament and the English Parliament formed the Solemn League and Covenant in 1643 with the aim to replace the Episcopacy of the Church of England with reformed teaching and practice. The civil war began in earnest. The commander-in-chief of the parliamentary army was Sir Thomas Fairfax. Oliver Cromwell was the cavalry general. Oliver Cromwell distinguished himself in the battle of Marston Moor in 1644. The army was reorganised as the New Model Army by Cromwell. Cromwell's discipline and strategies proved decisive. He was a man who feared God and was zealous for public liberty. He surrounded himself with men of prayer and personally led his men into battle. Archbishop Laud was imprisoned by Parliament in 1641 and executed for treason by beheading in 1645. Due to his political intrigues, Charles I was executed as a traitor in 1649. Charles II escaped to France in 1650. Cromwell became the Lord Protector and ruled through Parliament.

The victory of Parliament brought a new set of problems. The Presbyterian majority in Parliament disliked and feared the army, in which the Independents dominated. There was unrest in the army due to unpaid wages. On 12 June 1643, Parliament passed a law calling for an assembly of learned and godly divines (scholars) to meet and settle the doctrine and practice of the Church of England. There were 151 nominated members, 121 of whom were ministers of England and Scotland, and 30 were laymen. They met at Westminster Abbey a total of 1,163 times up to 22 February 1649. The Assembly produced the Westminster Confession of Faith, the Larger and Shorter Catechisms, and the Directory of Public Worship. The Westminster Confession of Faith, published in 1647, broadly represented the theology of the Puritans – except on church government which was Presbyterian, and church membership which included the children of believers through infant sprinkling. After the death of Oliver Cromwell his son, Richard, replaced him as Lord Protector. He was not as capable a leader as his father. In 1660, Charles II returned to England to reign.

The period 1640 to 1660 was when Puritanism reached its apex, after which the number of gifted ministers declined. In 1662 an act was passed requiring strict conformity to the Church of England and the Book of Common Prayer. About 2,000 Puritans who refused to conform were ejected from the church. This caused much personal hardship. It also strengthened the cause of Nonconformity. Some scholars see the Great Ejection of 1662 as the beginning of the decline of Puritanism. Persecution of the Dissenters was severe and relentless. Nonconformists were barred from the universities and this had an adverse effect on the standards of the ministry. The unity that had encouraged the growth of the brotherhood of Puritan pastors declined after 1662. The last well-known Puritans who died were John Howe in 1705 and Thomas Doolittle in 1707.

The 1689 Confession

The Puritans were made up of Anglicans, Presbyterians, Congregationalists, and Baptists. There were two groups of Baptists. The General Baptists were Arminian in soteriology (the doctrine of salvation), which was a result of their close association with the Anabaptists in the founding years. The Particular Baptists were off-shoots of the Congregationalists, sharing the same form of church government but rejecting their infant sprinkling. The first Particular Baptist Confession was published in 1644 in England. It was revised in 1646 and presented to Parliament. It consists of 52 articles, is strongly Calvinist and clearly asserts believer's baptism by immersion. It also restricts the Lord's Supper to baptised believers.

The Congregationalists adopted the Westminster Confession of Faith with some amendments, in 1658, calling it the Savoy Declaration of Faith and Order. In 1677 an assembly of Particular Baptist pastors and elders met and produced their second and fuller Confession of Faith. It was not signed at this stage because Charles II was then on the British throne. It was a time of persecution for Nonconformists. The introduction to the 1677 edition stated that it is a modification of the Westminster Confession and also of the Savoy Declaration of Faith and Order, "to convince all that we have no itch to clog religion with new words, but do readily acquiesce in that form of sound words, which hath been in consent with the Holy Scripture, used by others before us." Twelve years after the Baptist Confession was drawn up by the persecuted ministers a new era of liberty dawned. In 1689 thirty-seven leading Baptist ministers reissued the Confession and it was circulated among the churches. In England and Wales it became the definitive Confession of the Particular or Calvinistic Baptist churches and remained so for the next two centuries. It is today referred to as 'the Second London Baptist Confession of Faith of 1689', or just 'the 1689 Confession" in short.

In 1742 the 1689 Confession was adopted by the Calvinistic Baptists of North America – with the addition of two short chapters entitled 'Of The Singing Of Psalms & Etc.' and 'Of Laying On Of Hands' – and called by them the Philadelphia Confession of Faith. In 1855, the youthful C. H. Spurgeon became minister of the New Park Street Chapel, London. In a few months only he determined to strengthen the doctrinal foundations of the churches by the re-issue of the Confession. He appended these words to the Confession: "This ancient document is the most excellent epitome of the things most surely believed among us. It is not issued as an authoritative rule or code of faith, whereby you may be fettered, but as a means of edification in righteousness. It is an excellent, though not inspired, expression of the teaching of those Holy Scriptures by which all confessions are to be measured. We hold to the humbling truths of God's sovereign grace in the salvation of lost sinners. Salvation is through Christ alone and by faith alone"

In 1958, the year when revival of interest in Reformed theology really began to accelerate, the Confession was republished. Further editions came in 1963, 1966, 1970 and 1974. In 1975 Erroll Hulse, through Carey Publications, published 'A Faith To Confess', being the 1689 Confession rewritten in modern English by S. M. Houghton, together with a useful introduction. Further editions of this came nearly every two years after that. In 1980, Gospel Mission Press in America republished the original Confession. In the same year, Metropolitan Tabernacle (Spurgeon's Church) in London published the Confession containing brief notes by Dr. Peter Masters. The 1689 Confession has been translated into different languages to cater to the needs of newly-planted Reformed Baptist churches throughout the world.

The Reformed Baptists are the spiritual descendants of the Particular Baptists. The change in name is deemed more appropriate in an age when the struggles are for the recovery of the full-orbed teaching of Scripture, as during the Reformation, rather than to distinguish between General and Particular Baptists, as in the age of the Puritans. In the providence of God, the Reformation occurred in Europe, leading to the rise of Puritanism in Britain, which then spread to Europe, North America, and now to other parts of the world. In the providence of God, the 1689 Confession was compiled by the Particular Baptists, building upon the earlier confessions and the distilled teaching of the Puritans and the Reformers.

We do not claim that the Reformers and the Puritans had everything right, in doctrine and practice. They were children of their times, and they were men "with a nature like ours" (cf. James 5:17). The Reformers disagreed over baptism and the Lord's Supper. The Puritans disagreed over the form of church government. Through their interaction with one another, they were seeking to know the correct teaching on these matters. The various confessions of faith that arose from the Reformation – including during the Puritan age – reflect these differences among them. It is left to us to be convinced from Scripture which is the most consistent scriptural teaching on theses matters. They, more than any group of the Lord's people in history, saw the teaching of Scripture clearly as a system of truth – "the faith which was once for all delivered to the saints (Jude 3)".

2.3   Implications

We must close with some implications for ourselves today.

1 *The succession of truth matters more than ecclesiastical pedigree or historical lineage.*

Doctrine governs practice. The Puritans have been called the second generation of Reformers because the held to the theology and spirit of the Reformation. The Reformation gave rise to the mainline Protestant churches in Continental Europe, including the Moravian Church, the Lutheran Church, the Dutch Reformed Church, and the Mennonite Church. Puritanism in Britain and New England gave rise to the Church of England which is Episcopal in church government, the Church of Scotland which is Presbyterian, the General Baptists who practise democratic congregationalism, the Congregationalists who practice Independency and hold to infant sprinkling, and the Particular Baptists who practise Independency but hold to believer's baptism. The Methodist Church came into being in in England and Wales in the 1740s, while the Plymouth Brethren Assemblies came into being in Ireland in the 1820s. Both the Methodists and the Plymouth Brethren have their roots in Anglicanism (i.e. the Church of England). All the mainline denominations may, therefore, claim historical lineage to the Reformation and Puritanism. However, most denominations today pay scant attention to Reformed and Puritan theology, and what they stood for, but prefer to be known only as Protestants or Evangelicals.

2 *It is naive not to learn from church history and the providence of God.*

Those who do not learn from church history are bound to repeat the mistakes of the past. Those who do not see divine providence ordering the events of the past will be blind to God's will for the present. As new churches are planted, the teaching of Scripture will need to be taught and applied more and more. The same issues faced by God's people in the past will surface – for example, the authority of Scripture, the doctrine of salvation, the doctrine of sanctification, public worship, church discipline and government, missions, inter-church relationship, the return of Christ, the day of judgement, and the like. We are not so much concerned about the shape of the church building, the ringing of the church bell, the celebration of Christmas, and the like. Our concern is with the teaching of Scripture, and its application to the life of the

Christian and the church. This is where the confessions of faith that arose from the Reformation are so helpful and beneficial.

3 *A confessional church will seek to glorify God in doctrine and practice.*
We believe that the Reformed faith is the closest expression of the system of teaching taught in the Scripture. The confessions of faith that arose from the Reformation are our tutors, to guide us to the correct understanding of the word of God. Of those confessions, the 1689 Confession is the most mature – having been built upon the previous confessions of faith and the distilled teaching of the Puritans and the Reformers. We commend the 1689 Confession to our friends and brethren. A confessional church will not merely pay lip-service to believing in a Confession of Faith. Instead, it will declare adherence to that Confession in the church Constitution, and seek to teach and practise what is taught in Scripture as expressed in the Confession.

4 *The spirit of the Reformation must be consistently pursued.*
Each generation has to face its own challenges. Each generation has its own battles to fight. The living and true God has given us the sword of the Spirit, which is the word of God (Eph. 6:17). He has promised us the abundance of power from the Holy Spirit to know His word and do His will (Eph. 3:14-21). We do not want to hold to the confession of faith merely as a tradition of the church, devoid of the spirit of the Reformers and the Puritans, which may be described as *semper reformanda* – 'always being reformed'. We must desire to know and do God's will in our generation, and not remain stagnant at where the Reformers and the Puritans left us. In the words of John Robinson (1575-1625), a leader of the early English Separatists, we are persuaded that "the Lord hath more truth yet to break forth out of His holy word."

2.4 Recommended Reading

1 Hulse, Erroll, 2000. Who Are The Puritans? Evangelical Press.

2 Poh, B. S. 2017. What is a Reformed Baptist Church? Good News Enterprise.

3 Poh, B. S. 2017. Thoroughgoing Reformation, Good News Enterprise.

Three

THE LEGITIMACY OF USING THE CONFESSION OF FAITH

A recovery of the Reformed Faith began in the 1960s in the United Kingdom and in the United States of America. It spread worldwide so that today there is a Reformed movement in many parts of the world. Older churches were revived, and newer churches have been planted. The Reformed churches are known for their emphasis on the authority of Scripture, the sovereignty of God, the Calvinistic system of salvation, the centrality of the local church, and the primacy of preaching. Another characteristic of the churches that are Reformed is the adherence to one of the confessions of faith that arose from the Reformation. In conjunction with adherence to a confession of faith, the Reformed churches frequently use catechisms to teach doctrine. Catechising is a time-tested method of instruction used in the Christian church, but it is largely unknown among the modern evangelical churches.

Reformed churches are creedal, believing in the legitimacy of setting forth their belief in a systematic way in documents which they call the confessions of faith. They stand in contrast to the many evangelical churches that are unsympathetic to any creed or statement of faith. In fact, there are many modern evangelicals who are antagonistic to any form of creedal Christianity. Their battle cry is "No creed but the Bible alone." They convey the impression that they have a concern to uphold the sole authority of Scripture, and imply that we, who are Reformed, are inconsistent in championing the sole authority of Scripture because we are introducing another source of authority next to the Bible.

So widespread is this anti-creedal sentiment that many unthinking Christians have been adversely influenced. They look upon Reformed people as queer and narrow-minded. Upon exposure to the Reformed faith, a number of them have become convinced of the truth. But they are still beset with the difficulty of reconciling the emphasis on the sole authority of Scripture, championed by Reformed people, and their adherence to the confession of faith. To their mind, the belief in the sole authority of Scripture automatically rules out any place for the confession of faith. Indeed, there are those who are prepared to call themselves Reformed but are reluctant to place any importance upon the confession of faith.

It seems right, therefore, that we should defend the legitimacy of using the confession of faith. This has been done by more able people before this. The need of the times, however, require that we continue to sound forth what we believe so that truth will finally prevail. We wish to help the struggling individuals to come all the way with us. We wish to strengthen those who are already with us so that they may be firmly established in the belief in the legitimacy of using the confession of faith.

3.1 Definitions

To help in our deliberation, we must clarify some terms and make some definitions. We all know that words can be used in the general sense, and they can also be used in the technical sense – they can be generic or specific. In books and articles, you often find all three terms 'creed', 'statement of faith', and 'confession of faith' used interchangeably to refer to the written beliefs of the church. I prefer to be more precise and will be using these terms in their specific senses, unless the context show otherwise.

By **creeds** I refer to the brief statements of faith drawn up by the early church to counter particular errors or heresies. Three well known creeds handed down to us are the Apostles' Creed, the Athanasian Creed, and the Nicene Creed. The Apostles' Creed seemed to have been drawn up in the second century to counter Gnosticism[1] and Docetism[2]. The Athanasian Creed is commonly thought to have been produced in the fourth or fifth century to counter Arianism[3]. The Nicene Creed was drawn up in AD 325 at the Council of Nicaea. It was revised by the Council of Constantinople (AD 381) and reaffirmed by the Council of Chalcedon (AD 451). As a more direct statement on the Trinity it became a test of the orthodoxy and competence of the clergy. All three creeds were valued highly by the Reformers. These creeds are accepted by, or acceptable to, all the Orthodox churches and all Protestant and evangelical churches today.

By *confessions of faith* I refer to the fuller statements of belief drawn up during and after the Reformation. By that time, the Orthodox churches – including the Roman Catholic, Syrian Orthodox, Greek Orthodox, Russian Orthodox, Egyptian Coptic, and Mar Thoma churches – have gone astray in many areas, including the doctrine of salvation and the manner of worship. During the Reformation, the Protestant churches found it necessary to distance themselves from these orthodox churches, and the Roman Catholic Church in particular. They also had to contend with Pelagianism[4] and Socinianism[5]. There were also differences on baptism, the Lord's Supper, the form of church government, and a host of other issues. The confessions of faith drawn up during the Reformation and the Puritan age were therefore more comprehensive, covering systematically the fundamental beliefs of the Christian faith.

By *statements of faith* I refer to the short statements drawn up by various evangelical churches in more recent years. Like the creeds of the early church, and unlike the confessions of faith of the Reformation, they are brief. Unlike the creeds of the early church, and

---

[1]Gnosticism taught that the world was created by a lesser divinity, called the 'demiurge', of whom Christ is an embodiment. To know the supreme being, enlightenment is need by special knowledge.

[2]Docetism taught that Christ was divine but did not have a real or natural body during His life on earth.

[3]Arianism taught that Christ was a created being, more than a man, but less than God.

[4]Pelagianism taught that original sin did not taint human nature and that humans have the free will to achieve human perfection without divine grace.

[5]Socinianism taught that there was no original sin, for humans were created mortal. It denied the deity of Christ and rejected the doctrine of the Trinity, holding instead to the belief that God is absolutely one.

like the confessions of faith of the Reformation, they cover a wide spectrum of doctrines. A typical statement of faith will include articles on the Scripture, the Godhead, salvation, sanctification, the church, the ordinances, and the future. The value of statements of faith is that they show in small compass the belief of the church so that a visitor may know that he is worshipping in a true church. The disadvantage is that they leave out too much so that it is impossible to judge the church on those areas that its statement of faith is silent about.

3.2 Legitimacy

We are now ready to consider the legitimacy of using the confession of faith. We need to note that the legitimacy, or rightness, of using the confession is different from the value of using it, although they overlap. We wish to consider why it is legitimate, or right, to use the confession. We will consider the value of using the confession after that.

There are two key passages of Scripture on which I base my arguments. The first is 1 Timothy 3:15, which says, "...but if I am delayed, I write so that you may know how you ought to conduct yourself in the house of God, which is the church of the living God, the pillar and ground of the truth." Here, the local church is regarded as the pillar and ground of the truth. The church has two basic responsibilities, the first of which is to hold up the truth like a pillar holding up the roof of a house. This speaks of the proclamational task of the church. When the truth is proclaimed, its light will shine far into the spiritual darkness of this world. Ignorance will be dispelled, doubts will be cleared, hearts will be convicted, and sinners will be drawn to faith in Christ. The second basic responsibility of the church is to build on the foundation of the truth. This speaks of the didactic task of the church. Once the gospel has brought about faith in the hearers, the whole counsel of God's word must be taught to them. Believers must grow in knowledge, in Christian graces, and in usefulness in the Lord's service.

The second passage to consider is Jude 3, which says. "Beloved, while I was very diligent to write to you concerning our common salvation, I found it necessary to write to you exhorting you to contend earnestly for the faith which was once for all delivered to the saints." Three points may be noted from this passage. Firstly, there is such a thing as "*the* faith" – the definite article is in the original Greek text. It is a definite faith, a definable faith, and not a vague, nebulous type of faith that has been handed down to us. Secondly, this definite and definable faith was "once for all delivered to the saints", which means that it has to be handed down to the subsequent generations of believers. We have a duty to pass on the faith to the future generations in such a way that the faith is not altered or adulterated. Thirdly, the faith must be contended for – and that earnestly, and not in a half-hearted way. In the original Greek, "to contend" is one word (*epagonizesthai*) which carries the idea of fighting and struggling against the enemies of the truth in order to preserve, uphold, and propagate it.

From these two key passages, we may draw out the following implications:

1 It is the duty of the church **to know, and define, the truth**. If the church does not know the truth, how can it teach it to others? If the truth cannot be clearly defined, how are the hearers to act? If the truth is not clearly stated, how are we to know what constitutes truth and what constitutes error? The trumpet that gives an unclear sound will not summon any one to battle. This is the first warrant for the confession of faith. Truth must be defined, which in practice means writing it down precisely, concisely, and comprehensively. When that is done, we have a confession of faith!

2 It is the duty of the church **to propagate the truth**. The gospel must be preached. The whole counsel of God's word must be taught. Faithful churches must be planted. The Great Commission is not an option but an imperative. What is the content of the gospel that we preach? What constitutes the whole counsel of God's word upon which we must establish the faith of believers? What sort of churches do we plant if we are not sure of the body of truth that constitutes "the faith"? The duty to propagate the truth is the second warrant for the confession of faith. Imagine sending your son out on an errant without spelling out clearly what he is expected to do. It will be like asking him to make bricks without giving him straw. This is exactly what happens when a church engages in preaching a message that it cannot clearly define. On

25

the other hand, when we define the message that is preached to sinners, and that is taught to believers, and on which churches are founded, we straightway have a confession of faith.

3 It is the duty of the church **to remain faithful**. Contrary to popular belief, faithfulness is not defined by the number of church members, nor by mere activity and enterprise. Instead, faithfulness is defined by doctrine and practice, in that number and in that order. Doctrine must come first, then practice. Without correct doctrine, there can be no correct practice. Correct doctrine alone does not make a church faithful, but obedience to the truth does. If Christians are to contend for the faith, they must themselves be faithful to that faith. In the second and third chapters of the book of Revelation, the churches that are not faithful in doctrine or practice are warned by the Lord and commanded to repent. It is not good enough to claim that you are correct on just a few main points, or even on most of the points of doctrine. We want to be correct in all points of doctrine, as far as is possible. The duty to remain faithful constitutes the third warrant for drawing up a confession of faith.

4 It is the duty of the church **to defend the faith**. Physical attacks upon the church from without is hard to bear, but it has the effect of cleansing the church. Doctrinal attacks from within the church is quiet and subtle, but it has the effect of destroying the whole church. The enemies of the gospel know that the more effective way to accomplish their objective is to infiltrate the church in order to bring about a slow but sure death. The apostle Paul warned the Ephesian elders of this danger in Acts 20:29-30, saying, "For I know this, that after my departure savage wolves will come in among you, not sparing the flock. Also from among yourselves men will rise up, speaking perverse things, to draw away the disciples after themselves." In his book "Doctrinal Integrity", Samuel Miller gave an interesting description of how the Council of Nicea attempted to ferret out the heresy of Arius on the divinity of Christ. Arius professed to believe in all that the Bible teaches about Christ, and was willing to accept all the language of the Bible concerning the person and nature of Christ. The Council finally formulated in their own language what they believed to be

the doctrine of Scripture on the divinity of Christ. Arius and his disciples refused to subscribe to the statement drawn up by the Council, so that it was discovered that all the while Arius held to a different understanding of the Scripture on the subject. That was a classic example of the necessity and value of a confession of faith. Imagine sending out soldiers to fight who are unable to distinguish the enemies from the friends! It is impossible to defend the faith without knowing and stating exactly what constitutes the faith.

5 The final point is that the church has a duty **to pass down the faith**. Here, we are referring to the passing on of the faith to the future generation. It is an accepted fact of life that we learn from those who are more knowledgeable than us so that we, in turn, can contribute to the knowledge. The source of our knowledge of God and His will is the Scripture. The Scripture is the complete and sufficient revelation of God to us. What we know from the Scripture must be passed on to the future generations so that they, in turn, can study deeper into the Scripture and pass on the faith. Since the confession of faith consists of doctrines laid out systematically in a concise and precise manner, it is the best 'frame of reference' for studying the Scripture. It is not as thick and unwieldy as a tome on systematic theology. It is not filled with discussions on disputable details. It only contains the fundamentals of the faith delineated with clarity.

We have covered five reasons why it is right to use the confession of faith. It is legitimate to use the confession of faith because: (i) the church has a duty to know and define the truth; (ii) the church has a duty to propagate the truth; (iii) the church has a duty to remain faithful to God; (iv) the church has a duty to defend the faith; and (v) the church has a duty to pass down the faith.

3.3   Value

We come now to consider the value of using the confession of faith. As mentioned already, the value of using the confession overlaps with the legitimacy of its use. Here, we will mention five specific advantages of using the confession of faith.

First, the confession of faith is a useful tool *for preparing believers for church membership*. The 1689 Baptist Confession of Faith consists of 32 chapters. We have been able to study two chapters in a half-an-hour session each week, so that the whole confession is covered within four months. An alternative approach which takes less time is to assign the prospective member to read through the confession of faith, after which one or two sessions can be held to discuss any points that are in doubt. We have made it a practice to study through the confession of faith in pioneering situations to prepare the believers for covenanting together as a church.

Second, the confession of faith is a useful standard *for maintaining the unity and purity of the church*. Membership in a church is a voluntary matter in which there is mutual agreement between the parties concerned to uphold the rules and regulations, as well as the belief, of the church. When any member departs from the doctrines set forth in the doctrinal standard, he is obliged to resign from membership after all due attempts have been made to sort out the difference. He may then join himself to another church that holds to doctrines that best accord with his new belief. The member should not insist on staying on as a member to stir up strife over his difference in doctrine, nor should he bear with the difference such that his conscience, or that of the members of the church, is hurt. In many situations, the person need only resign from membership while continuing to worship together with the church, until a better arrangement can be made.

Third, the confession of faith is a useful standard by which *to determine the suitability of candidates for the ministry*. Each local church has the right to determine who should be its pastor, just as each family has the right to determine who to take in as a lodger. A church will have not much problem with one from its own membership who is being considered for the ministry, but difficulty will arise if the candidate is from another church. Apart from matters of character and gifts, the candidate must be examined with regard to his belief to ensure that he upholds the doctrinal standard of the church.

Fourth, the confession of faith is useful *in determining the degree of fellowship we can have with another church or preacher*. We have to engage in selective fellowship because of limited time, resources, and opportunities. Furthermore, in a highly mobile age like ours, preachers often pass our way and seek opportunities to preach. It helps to know that the church or preacher professes adherence to one of the confessions of faith of the Reformation, although that is still no guarantee that he is truly sound in doctrine or safe in character and behaviour. Of course, we will be overjoyed to know a preacher or a church that holds to the same belief and practice as we do.

Fifth, the confession of faith *gives a sense of purpose and historical continuity to the church.* It has been our practice to avoid planting a church too near to another Reformed church, out of deference to it. We will certainly not plant a church right next door to a Reformed Baptist church. We are not in the business of competing with other churches, much less to engage in rivalry with a like-minded church. Our primary concern is to carry out the Great Commission – to preach the gospel and to found faithful churches. However, on some occasions we find ourselves planting a church where there are other churches already. The question may be asked, "How do we justify such a move?" Our answer is twofold. Firstly, the need for the gospel in that place is great, for the combined effort of all the churches there has hardly reached to ten percent of the population. You will find that that is true in nearly every such situation. Secondly, we believe it is justifiable to provide an alternative to the teaching given by the other non-Reformed churches. As we are able, we will interact with the other churches to help them come to a better understanding of the truth, but we must not be held back in the task of propagating what we believe to be the truth. Each church, and each Christian, will have to answer to the Lord on the last day. Our own church members know that we have close fellowship with other like-minded churches, and they know that we stand in a long line of believers who have held to the same truth in times past. Our fellowship with believers at the present, and in the past, is based on truth.

3.4 Objections

Having covered the legitimacy and value of using the confession of faith, it is a small matter to counter the objections raised by our opponents. What are the common objections that have been raised against the use of the confession of faith? There are four.

First, it is claimed that the use of the confession of faith is **contrary to our belief in the sole authority of Scripture**. That is not the case, however, for anyone who cares to read our confession of faith will find it clearly affirming that Scripture alone is the authority in all matters of faith and practice. The 1689 Baptist Confession of Faith opens with the this statement: "The Holy Scripture is the only sufficient, certain, and infallible rule of all saving knowledge, faith, and obedience (1:1)." It goes on to affirm that, "The whole counsel of God concerning all things necessary for his own glory, man's salvation, faith and life, is either expressly set down or necessarily contained in the Holy Scripture, to which nothing at any time is to be added, whether by new revelation of the Spirit, or traditions of men (1:6)."

The confession of faith is certainly not a subordinate authority, much less is it another authority equal to Scripture. The Holy Scripture is our only authority. We do not use the confession of faith to interpret the Scripture. The confession is our interpretation of the Scripture. It is therefore the doctrinal standard of our church. Any apparent authority attached to the confession of faith is derived from the Scripture, since it contains the teaching of Scripture. Put another way, the confession of faith has no original authority, independent of Scripture.

This leads us to the second objection, which is that the use of the confession of faith is **against the liberty of conscience**. The claim is that we are making it obligatory to all who wish to join our church to subscribe to our interpretation of the Scripture. But that is not the case, for our confession of faith also affirms the belief in the liberty of conscience. It says, "God alone is Lord of the conscience, and has left it free from the doctrines and commandments of men which are in any thing contrary to his word, or not contained in it (21:2)." We may teach and persuade people to consider becoming members of the church, but they must do it voluntarily. If they do not believe in the doctrines set forth in our confession of faith, we are not willing to accept them into membership. Just as we respect their right to act according to their belief, so too they must respect our right as a church to act according to our belief.

The third objection is that adherence to the confession of faith **stifles our understanding of the truth**. The claim is that we are hemmed in by the confession of faith so that we become narrow-minded and are no longer open to other views. Our answer is that the confession of faith has instilled in us a high regard for the Scripture and a strong desire to know more of the truth. As we are driven to study the Scripture, we become convinced all the more that the fundamentals of the faith as set forth in the confession are right, in contrast to the views propagated by others. We have never treated the confession of faith as sacrosanct, and acknowledge that in some points, there are genuine differences of opinion. For example, among those who hold to the 1689 Baptist Confession of Faith, there is disagreement on whether the pope is the final antichrist or just a manifestation of the many antichrists who foreshadow the coming final one. There is also disagreement on whether all infants who die are elect, and therefore saved, or only the elect among the infants who die are saved. It may be observed that the champions of the faith – the great preachers, theologians, and missionaries – have come largely from the rank of those who hold to the confessions of faith.

The final objection is that adherence to the confession of faith tends to *stifle fellowship between churches*. It is claimed that Reformed people tend to keep to themselves, and are not at liberty to have fellowship with all and sundry. Our answer is that that is a matter of our choice. We are at liberty to choose who we have fellowship with, and the chief criterion for fellowship is agreement on the truth. The more truth we are agreed upon, the closer is our fellowship, and vice versa. We practise selective fellowship because, in obedience to the Lord, we cannot have fellowship with the purveyors of heresies and have to withdraw from brethren who erred from the truth. (See Romans 16:17-18; 2 John 7-11; and 2 Thessalonians 3:6, 14-15.) This is not to say that we think ourselves to be the only true and faithful Christians around, for we do acknowledge that many Christians who differ from us often show a true love for the Lord and serve Him zealously. With such, we will have no difficulty in fellowship.

3.5   Which Confession?

By this time, I hope you are convinced that it is legitimate, and to our advantage, to use the confession of faith. The final matter we wish to consider is which confession of faith we should adopt.

Reformed churches are realistic in their approach to this matter. It is not impossible to draw up a confession of faith that is totally new. However, the effort will be a colossal one, for the proposed confession of faith must be accurate and acceptable to all who are of like faith. It will be difficult to summon together enough like-minded and capable people to sit at conference for a sustained period, to thoroughly accomplish the task from scratch. In the providence of God, the Reformation took place with the result that a number of good confessions of faith have been drawn up. The men involved in drawing up the confessions were eminently qualified in terms of scholarship, piety, and experience. The confessions drawn up by them have been tested and tried through the centuries. Why not use them instead of attempting to re-invent the wheel?

Let me briefly introduce to you some of these confessions of faith. Four well-known confessions of faith are the following:

The Three Forms of Unity (comprising the Heidelberg Cate- chism, the Belgic Confession, and the Canons of Dort), which was drafted in 1561/63 and reaffirmed in 1618/19, is the confession of faith of many Reformed churches on the continent of Europe, and of their offspring in America and other parts of the world.

The Westminster Confession of Faith, produced by the West- minster divines in Britain in 1647, is adopted by many Presbyterian churches throughout the world today.

The Savoy Declaration of Faith and Order, produced in Eng- land in 1658, is the confession of faith of the Congregationalists.

The 1689 Baptist Confession of Faith, produced anonymously by the persecuted Particular Baptists in Britain in 1677, and re-issued publicly in 1689, is today used by Reformed Baptists worldwide.

There are other confessions of faith that came from the Reforma- tion, including *the Separatist Confession of 1596, the 1644 Confes- sion of Faith of the Particular Baptists, the 1678 Orthodox Creed of the General Baptists*, and *the Forty-nine Articles of the Church of England*.

All these confessions of faith are Calvinistic in soteriology, except the Orthodox Creed of the General Baptist, which is Arminian. They differ from one another mainly in the form of church government. The Forty-nine Articles of the Church of England is prelatical and Erastian – believing in an hierarchy of individuals ruling over the churches, with the queen (or king) as the governor (or head) of the church. The Three Forms of Unity and the Westminster Confession of Faith advocate the Presbyterian form of church government, in which there is an hierarchy of committees ruling over the churches. The Savoy Declaration of Faith and the 1689 Baptist Confession of Faith both advocate the Independent form of church government, in which the churches are autonomous – ruled by elders, with congregational consent. The 1689 Baptist Confession of Faith differ from all the other confessions in that it upholds the baptism of believers by immersion.

Which of these should you adopt for your churches? That is for you to decide. You will need to come to your own conclusion on the differences reflected in the different confessions of faith. Here, we will practise true liberty of conscience, and mutually respect those who differ from us. I would only appeal to you to be absolutely honest in the study of these issues, and not be controlled by human traditions or personal prejudice.

3.6 Conclusion

In conclusion let us be reminded that the adoption a confession of faith is no indication that the church is faithful, neither is it a guarantee that it will not go astray. The Church of England, and many Presbyterian churches throughout the world, profess adherence to their respective confessions of faith, but do not truly value nor teach the truths contained in them. We do not regard such churches as truly Reformed. In order to be truly obedient to the Lord, and to avoid straying from the faith, we must embrace the confession of faith sincerely and put into practice its truths. We live in an age of doctrinal relativism, and it behoves those who love the truth to stand firm on the confession of faith. Indeed, we must not operate on the defensive, believing in the legitimacy and usefulness of the confession of faith, but rather, go on the offensive and show our opponents the imperative of being confessional in order to prove their fidelity to Scripture.

3.7 References

1 Martin, Robert Paul. The Legitimacy and Use of Confessions, in A Modern Exposition of the 1689 Baptist Confession of Faith, Evangelical Press (1989).

2 Miller, Samuel. 1989. Doctrinal Integrity, by Samuel Miller, Presbyterian Heritage Publications.

Four

THE SUBSCRIPTION DEBATE AND ITS RELEVANCE

Standing by itself, the title of this article means nothing to a lot of people. I suspect that after being told it has something to do with the Confession of Faith, many will still be in the dark as to what the topic is all about. This is the case even among Reformed Christians who hold to a Confession of Faith. Although the Subscription Debate is not widely known, it is nevertheless an important issue. This is so because, if it is not settled, it will sooner or later affect the peace and unity of a church, and of any grouping of Reformed churches. The events and circumstances surrounding the spread of the Reformed faith in recent years indicate that the issue is alive and affecting the people concerned, without it being recognised as such. I believe that this issue will be pressed upon us more and more in the days ahead, and we do well to be familiar with it.

From the outset, it needs to be noted that the Subscription Debate concerns the confessional Christians and churches. It is not the concern of Christians and churches that are non-confessional.

Here. I will address the issue in three parts. In the first part, I will give some definitions. In the second part, I will provide a sketch of the Debate. In the third and last part, I will discuss the relevance of the debate to us today.

4.1 Definitions

The first question we will try to answer is, "What is the Subscription Debate?" The Subscription Debate is a controversy in Presbyterian circles concerning the degree and extent of commitment to the doctrinal standards of the church. The controversy began in Britain in the 17th century, spread to North America in the 18th century, and resurfaced in the 19th century. At the end of the twentieth century, it surfaced yet again, and agitated the Presbyterian churches. Although the issue appeared academic, it had direct practical implications – affecting the ordination of ministers, church membership, and the fellowship between otherwise like-minded churches. The controversy polarised around two views of subscription to the doctrinal standards of the church, namely the Westminster Confession of Faith, the Shorter Catechism, and the Larger Catechism.

What is subscription to a doctrinal standard? What does it mean when someone says that he subscribes to a confession of faith? It means that he believes in the doctrines set forth in that confession of faith. It means that he is committed personally to those doctrines. Straightway, two questions arise. What degree of commitment does he have to those doctrines? And what extent of the doctrine of that confession of faith does he commit himself to? He may mean that his commitment is to all the doctrines of the confession, or to 80 percent of the doctrine, or to the main doctrines contained in it. If he means the main doctrines of the confession of faith, another question will arise, namely, which constitute the main doctrines? We will leave this last question for later. For the moment, we will concentrate on the degree of commitment and the extent of doctrine that is committed to.

Normally, a Presbyterian minister makes two vows at his ordination. The first ordination vow reads, "Do you believe the Scriptures of the Old and New Testament, as originally given, to be the inerrant word of God, the infallible rule of faith and practice?" Other Reformed churches will have a similar, if not exactly the same, vow. There is no room for any loose subscription here. Anyone who cannot take this vow with a clear conscience, sincerely, and wholeheartedly, is not fit to be the pastor of a Reformed church.

The second ordination vow of the Presbyterian minister reads, in part, "Do you sincerely receive and adopt the Confession of Faith and the Catechisms of this church, as containing the system of doctrine taught in the Holy Scriptures;..." It is here that differences arise. *Strict or full subscription* requires that he takes at face value the second ordination vow. The vow requires the adoption of the Confession of Faith and Catechisms, no more and no less, believing that they contain the system of doctrine taught in the Scriptures.

Before proceeding further, let us note some things that strict or full subscription does not mean. First, it does not insist that all of the teachings of the Confession and Catechisms are of equal importance, just as not all the teachings in the Bible are of equal importance. The full subscriptionist recognises that some doctrines are fundamental compared to others. Second, full subscription does not require the adoption of every word of the Confession and Catechisms. Instead, it requires the adoption of every doctrine or teaching of the Confession and Catechisms. Third, full subscription does not mean placing the Confession and Catechisms on the same level as the Bible. Instead, the Confession and Catechisms are made the doctrinal standards of the church because what they say are true to the Bible.

The second view is known as *loose or system subscription*. It maintains that we subscribe to a system of doctrine which is not specifically defined, but which is contained in the Confession and Catechisms of the church. The loose subscriptionist maintains that only the doctrines comprising the system are covered in the words of the second ordination vow. Doctrines that are not part of the system are not included. It is left to the courts of the church, as occasion arises, to define which doctrines are essential parts of the system of doctrine. This means that the system has not been settled.

We see now the contrast between the two views. The Full Subscription position holds that we subscribe to the Confession and Catechisms because they contain the doctrines of the Bible, whereas the Loose Subscription position holds that we subscribe only in so far as these documents contain doctrines of the Bible. It would seem that the loose subscriptionist is trying to avoid the danger of elevating the uninspired Confession and Catechisms to the level of the Bible – a danger which the full subscriptionist strenuously avoids, and has never been guilty of. The loose subscriptionist fails to see that, noble though his intention may be, his position leaves open the possibility of other men abusing it, which in fact has happened in history. The Loose Subscription position does not fix the boundary of the system of doctrine contained in the doctrinal standards, allowing for its proponent to regard certain doctrines as not essential to the system, and therefore not requiring his commitment to them. The degree of his commitment to the doctrinal standards of the church becomes relative. This is not the case with the Full Subscription position, which requires full commitment to all the doctrines set forth in the doctrinal standards of the church.

There is, in fact, a third position, which identifies the Confession of Faith with the teaching of the Bible. This rigid position virtually places the Confession of Faith on the same level with the Bible – both are of equal authority. Our interest here is not with this position, but with the two mentioned earlier.

As I understand it, we may represent the two positions by the diagram below:

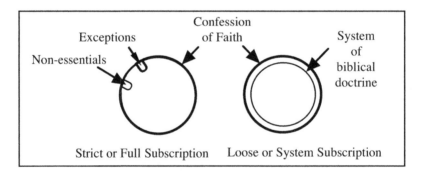

Fig. 4.1 Strict And Loose Subscription

In the Strict or Full Subscription position, we have the circle which represents the Confession of Faith – and, to the Presbyterian Church, it includes the two Catechisms. The Confession is regarded as containing the system of doctrine taught in the Bible. We shall say something about the "exceptions" and the "non-essentials" later. At this point, we need only to take note of the main difference between the Full and the Loose Subscription positions.

In the Loose Subscription position, there is a circle representing the Confession of Faith. The loose subscriptionist does not hold to the Confession of Faith as containing the system of doctrine of the Bible. Instead, he holds to the system of doctrine which he believes to be biblical, as contained in the Confession of Faith. To the loose subscriptionist, therefore, the boundary of the system he believes to be biblical is not fixed.

It needs to be noted that the doctrine of many loose subscriptionists actually coincides with that of the full subscriptionists. However, since the Loose Subscription position has no fixed boundary for the biblical doctrine, it opens itself to other men who may say that they hold to the system of doctrine contained in the Confession of Faith, but leave out too much of what is contained in the Confession of Faith.

We should now be clear as to what is the Subscription Debate, what it means to subscribe to the doctrinal standards of the church, what the Full and Loose Subscription positions believe in, respectively, and the issue that is at stake in the debate. We shall now proceed to give a brief sketch of the history of the debate, so that the practical implications are fully appreciated.

4.2   A Sketch Of The Controversy

The controversy began in Britain. The Westminster Assembly, called by Parliament to draw up the doctrinal standards for the churches in Britain, was divided over the issue of subscription. The Assembly did not settle the issue, but left this to Parliament. In Scotland, the General Assembly adopted the Westminster Confession in 1645. The Presbytery in Ulster, Northern Ireland, followed suit and also adopted it.

Required subscription to the Confession and Catechisms was not enacted in Scotland until 1690. It was further strengthen by a series of enactment between 1690 and 1700. We do not agree that the state should enact on matters pertaining to the doctrine of the church, but the fact was that the Church of Scotland was now placed in the position to enforce the requirement of full subscription to its doctrinal standards. The church, however, did not enforce it. Instead, liberal and heretical professors were tolerated in its fold so that their influence became pervasive. This led to the Secession of 1733.

In Ireland, particularly Northern Ireland, full subscription to the Westminster Standards began in 1697. As in Scotland, this was not strictly enforced. Eventually the church in Ireland was rocked by the subscription controversy, in which the issue was whether subscription was right or wrong. The church became divided between the Subscribers and the Non-subscribers. The Presbyterians around Belfast, with English and not Scottish roots, were generally non-subscribers. They were so lax as to say that the deity of Christ was not necessary. One's conscience and not the Bible or any confessional statement was to be the rule of life and practice. This led to the expulsion of the non-subscribing churches in 1726. By that time, the damage had been done. Around that time a great many of the Scotch-Irish emigrated to America, who became a predominant force in the Presbyterian Church in America.

We now shift our attention to America. The first Presbyterian Church was established in America in 1706. In 1729, a full synod was called in which the Adopting Act was passed, which required full subscription to the Westminster Standards. The Adopting Act required full subscription to the Confession and Catechisms, except for some clauses of the twentieth and twenty-third chapters, concerning the power of the civil magistrate over synods, and power to prosecute any for their religion. The exception clause was to lead to further debate on what the allowance of an exception means, which is of relevance to us today. In the years following, the issue of whether it was permissible for a full subscriptionist to express his scruples over non-fundamental matters was raised. The concept of stating scruples is also relevant to us today. These we shall discuss later.

Let us come back to our sketch of the debate in America. We are now moving into the 19th century. In 1801, the Presbyterian Church and the Congregational Churches of Connecticut merged under a Plan of Union. The Plan allowed for individuals to be seated in the Congregations, Presbyteries, Synods, and General Assembly without the requirement of subscription. When the demand was made for subscription, the question of what was involved was raised. A school of "loose" subscriptionists arose, who argued that all that was being accepted was the system of doctrine, not the Confession and Catechisms themselves, as containing that system taught in the Scriptures. This in effect, nullified subscription to the Standards, since this so-called "system of doctrine" was not defined. The conflict between the Old School Presbyterians and the New School Presbyterians came to its climax when the Old School party took firm control of the Assembly in 1837, and cut off all congregations, presbyteries, and synods that had been formed on the basis of the Plan of Union. It has generally been held that the New School Church, with its loose subscription, led to the introduction of liberalism into the Presbyterian Church.

In the last decade of the twentieth century, the debate resurfaced, this time touching the ordination vow of the minister. The issue involved in the debate is clearly set forth in the book, "The Subscription Debate", by Morton H. Smith, from which the historical material of this talk is taken. The issue included the questions: Is it required of the minister to be a full subscriptionist? If so, is any scruples over non-essential doctrines allowed? If allowed, how do we handle them?

Our sketch of the history of the Subscription Debate must end here, brief though it has been. One obvious point from this sketch is that the Debate had such serious practical implications – affecting the unity and peace of the church, the communion of churches, the admission of members of the church, and the appointment of ministers.

We shall now consider the relevance of the Debate to us.

4.3 Relevance

The biblical basis

From all that has been said thus far, you would have gathered that I am a full subscriptionist, who is advocating the full subscription position. I believe that it is essential for every serious Christian to subscribe fully to the confession of faith of his church. Speaking from the perspective of a Reformed Baptist, I would not insist on including the catechism in the doctrinal standard of the church, although we value highly, and do make much use of, the catechism. The 1689 Confession of Faith is sufficiently comprehensive to clearly define the biblical system of truth. Each church will have to decide on its own doctrinal standard.

What is the biblical basis for holding to the full subscription position? I would say that the arguments I gave to prove the legitimacy of using the confession of faith, based on I Timothy 3:15 and Jude 3, are equally applicable in providing the biblical basis for the full subscription position. Let me summarise the arguments here. The church is "the pillar and ground of the truth". It is required of us "to contend earnestly for the faith which was once for all delivered to the saints". From these, we may draw out the following implications: it is the duty of the church to know and define the truth; it is the duty of the church to propagate the truth; it is the duty of the church to remain faithful; it is the duty of the church to defend the faith; it is the duty of the church to pass down the faith. We need to notice that the assumption of a definite and definable system of truth has been made, without which those duties of the church will become meaningless. Is it not meaningless for us to have a duty to know and define the truth when the truth cannot be clearly defined? Is it not meaningless to defend the faith when that faith cannot be clearly defined? Is it not meaningless to pass down the faith when that faith cannot be clearly stated?

We may garner further biblical arguments in support of the full subscription position. In Acts 20:27 the apostle Paul says, "For I have not shunned to declare to you the whole counsel of God." Note that it is the whole counsel of God, not a partial counsel of God, that has been declared. Our subscription is to the confession of faith as a whole, which we believe contains the system of truth taught in the Bible, and not to some vague system of truth that is less than what is taught in the confession.

In 2 Timothy 1:13 the same apostle says, "Hold fast the pattern of sound words which you have heard from me, in faith and love which are in Christ Jesus." Then, in 2 Timothy 2:2 he says, "And the things that you have heard from me among many witnesses, commit these to faithful men who will be able to teach others also." The expression, "the pattern of sound words" speaks of a definite body of truth, which has to be passed down to the future generations. This is in keeping with Jude 3, which we have already referred to: "...contend earnestly for the faith which was once for all delivered to the saints". Jude's readers knew what he meant by "the faith". This cannot be a reference to the subjective faith of the Christian, because the definite article is attached to the word "faith". Furthermore, a subjective faith can hardly be passed down without the presence of an objective body of truth called "the faith".

Exceptions

I trust what has been said is sufficient to convince you that the Full Subscription position is right. Now, we need to say something about the scruples of some full subscriptionists to certain articles in the Confession of Faith that may be regarded as not necessary or essential to the position of Full Subscription. We have noted earlier that full subscription does not mean that all of the teachings of the Confession are of equal importance. Furthermore, full subscription does not require the adoption of every word of the Confession. Instead, it requires the adoption of every doctrine or teaching of the Confession.

We consider first the case of a church consciously making exceptions of certain articles in the Confession of Faith. Presbyterians in many parts of the world have omitted certain articles in chapters 20 and 23 of the Westminster Confession of Faith, concerning the power of the civil magistrate, as necessary and essential to full subscription. Among the Reformed Baptists, the articles in the 1689 Confession of Faith that may be regarded as not necessary or essential to full subscription include the following:

i Equating the pope as "that antichrist, that man of sin, and that son of perdition, who exalts himself in the church against Christ, and all that is called God, whom the Lord shall destroy with the brightness of His coming (26:4)". From exegetical ground, many Reformed Baptists are not prepared to identify the pope as the particular antichrist of the end time. Instead, they look upon the pope, and the papal system, as one of the forerunners of the antichrist, who is yet to be revealed.

ii "Infants dying in infancy are regenerated and saved by Christ through the Spirit, who works when, where, and how He pleases (10:3)." Not all Reformed Baptists believe that all infants dying in infancy are saved. Instead, many believe that only those who are elect among the infants who die in infancy are saved. (When the Confession was first issued in 1677, the word "elect" was placed before "infants" so that the sentence reads, "Elect infants dying in infancy are regenerated and saved..." The sentence and its meaning parallel the next sentence, which reads, "So also are all elect persons who are incapable of being outwardly called by the ministry of the word.")

iii The ordination of elders to be done "by fasting and prayer, with the laying on of the hands of the eldership of the church, if there be any previously constituted." And the ordination of deacons to be done "by prayer, with the laying on of hands (26:9)". Some churches omit fasting and the laying of hands in these ordinations.

iv The necessity of churches to be united into regional associations so that when there are disputes the "many churches holding communion together do, through their messengers, meet to consider, and give their advice about the matter in dispute, and to report to all the churches concerned (26:15)." Quite many confessional Reformed Baptist churches do not believe in the formal association of churches, and interpret this section as referring to churches in loose fellowship with one another and meeting together to settle disputes as and when necessary. The language of this section, however, quite obviously refers to the formal association of churches. Moreover, the Confession of Faith was issued by the Particular Baptists of the seventeenth century who practised the regional association of churches.

v The manner of keeping the Lord's Day, which some think is a little too rigidly specified, viz. "The Sabbath is kept holy unto the Lord when men, after a due preparing of their hearts and ordering their common affairs beforehand, not only observe a holy rest all day – from their own works, words and thoughts, as well as their worldly employment and recreations – but are occupied throughout that day in the public and private acts of worship, and in the duties of necessity and mercy (22:8)." However, the three broad categories of activity mentioned – i.e. acts of piety (worship), necessity, and mercy – are a good guide to how the day is to be kept. The emphasis on keeping the day holy is in accordance to Scripture and consistent with the teaching of this chapter of the Confession, although one need not be too scrupulous over when the day begins and when the day ends.

Except for the above five matters, I doubt that there are seriously confessional Reformed Baptists who would treat other matters in the 1689 Confession as not necessary or essential to full subscription. It is the prerogative of the individual church to decide which of these matters are not necessary or essential. However, when there is departure from the overall thrust of any chapter of the Confession, it is no longer possible to claim adherence to that Confession. The church should amend the Confession to suit its own position and call that confession of faith by a different name. In our own church, and all the churches that we have planted, under God, only the first of these is treated as not necessary and not essential. We therefore declare in our Church Constitution our adherence to the 1689 Confession, with this clause excepted.

It has been mooted in certain Reformed Baptist circles that a revision of the 1689 Confession should be made, including fairly major amendments to articles other than those mentioned earlier, e.g. those that concern the covenants and the form of church government. In recent years there has been a controversy among Reformed Baptists over the doctrine of the church eldership and the manner of exercising rule. The proposed amendments on these issues are significant enough to alter the character of the original Confession of Faith. We are not talking about making *exceptions* of certain points in the Confession. We are talking about making *amendments* to the Confession such that the content of a chapter is altered significantly. I am not totally opposed to the idea of making such amendments, for I do not believe that the Confession is sacrosanct or perfect. However, such an amended Confession, if ever it is produced, should be called by a totally different name instead of retaining its original name or a semblance of it. This is to avoid confusion, and to be fair to the majority of other Reformed Baptist churches that are content to use the original Confession. When the Calvinistic Baptists in America made some minor amendments to the 1689 Confession in 1744, they called it by a totally different name, namely "The Philadelphia Confession of Faith".

To help us crystallise what we have learned thus far, let us look at the diagram again. We have seen that the Loose Subscription position holds to a system of doctrine which is believed to be biblical, which is contained in the Confession of Faith. This position is open to the possibility of someone saying, "I believe in the system of teaching taught in the Confession of Faith", when he actually believes less than, or differently from, what we believe to be contained in the Confession of Faith.

In the Full Subscription position, we say that we subscribe to the Confession of Faith as containing the system of doctrine taught in the Bible. We are not saying that we hold to all the wordings of the Confession, nor that all the doctrines of the Bible are equally important. Along the way, there are certain exceptions which we make, and we declare what they are. That way, other people will know that we hold to the Confession of Faith, with these exceptions.

Furthermore, we allow for the possibility that there may be those who are of our position – who are full subscriptionists – who may hold to more, or less, exceptions. We allow for the fact that they may have certain scruples over what may be called the non-essentials. The non-essentials, of course, are not fixed. It is up to the individual church to determine what constitute the non-essentials. This is so different from the Loose Subscription position.

Implications

Let us now consider how full subscriptionism impinges on church membership, the fellowship between churches, and the appointment of pastors. We begin with church membership. A church that holds to full subscription of the Confession will require its members to be full subscriptionists. This position is contrary to popular opinion to-day, for the non-confessional churches will only make salvation the only criterion of membership. Confessional churches believe that each church has a right, and a duty, to define the system of truth it believes to be biblical. This must not be understood to mean that we require every prospective member to be a theologian – knowing all the intricacies involved in every doctrine contained in the Confession. If we do so, we can rightly be charged with going beyond the requirement of Scripture for membership. We are fully aware that most new Christians do not know all the doctrines in depth. However, that is different from saying that they do not need to know and accept all the doctrines of the Confession. A new believer has known enough of the truth to be converted. Being genuinely regenerate, there will be a desire and willingness to learn more. In seeking to join the membership of the church, he should subscribe to the Confession, even though his understanding of the doctrines in the Confession may be very rudimentary. In fact, it will be beneficial to the church – for its peace, unity, and stability – to require the prospective member to attend a membership class in which the Confession is taught.

What happens if the member in due course grows in understanding and begins to have scruples over certain articles of the Confession? Is it required of him to resign from the membership? The answer will depend on whether the articles he has scruples over are regarded by the church as essential and necessary. The eldership of the church bears the responsibility of leading the church to a clear stand. The matter scrupled over must not be such as to overthrow the distinctives, or fundamentals, of that particular church – in its doctrine, worship, and government. For example, a Baptist church differs from a Presbyterian church on baptism. This difference should not be regarded as so serious as to prevent fellowship between the two churches. However, the warrant of existence of these churches as Baptist or Presbyterian lies in this difference, apart from other things. It is the right of a Reformed Baptist church to require adherence to believer's baptism – in belief and practice – as a criterion of membership. In other words, the issue of believer's baptism is a non-negotiable. It is essential and necessary to full subscription of its Confession. The member whose conviction on this issue has changed is obliged to resign amicably and join himself to a church that suits his new conviction. Of course, he may remain with the church after resigning, and willingly request for the spiritual oversight of the church, while serving in, and enjoying whatever privileges extended to him by, that church. On his part, he must not create strife over the difference, or chaff at the teaching and practice of the church.

We consider a slightly different situation, in which the prospective member is not a new believer, who comes with some fixed convictions of his own. If the difference in his conviction concerns a distinctive of the church, he should not be accepted into membership. This is because the Confession of Faith of the church is the uniting bond among its members, and the acceptance of this person will be a breach of full subscription.

47

What if the difference is over a matter that is regarded as not essential or necessary to full subscription? A common example is differences over whether infants dying in infancy are saved (10:3 of the Confession). If the particular church holds this article as not essential or necessary to full subscription, the member may remain in membership, and the prospective member may be accepted into membership. The member must be prepared to accept the position of the church on the issue, and all legitimate means adopted by the church to change his view.

We consider next the fellowship between churches. Churches that come together in formal association should agree on what constitute the exceptions to full subscription in that association. Differences may be allowed among the member churches over these exceptions. The situation is different in the case of an association which includes churches that are full subscriptionist and churches that are loose subscriptionist. Such an association will not remain united for long. It is far better to have an association of full subscriptionist churches which allows for the presence of messengers from the loose subcriptionist churches as observers. What if the loose subscriptionist churches choose to have their own association? That is their prerogative, over which we will not quarrel. My aim in this article has been to persuade you to adopt the full subscription position. But you may protest and say, "Aren't you precipitating a division between the full subscriptionists and the loose subscriptionists?" My answer is that we are not precipitating, but anticipating, a division. It is far better to begin with a firm foundation than to attempt to work together with a shaky foundation, for sooner or later a division will occur.

What of the loose fellowship between churches that are not in formal association? The degree of fellowship between them is directly proportional to the truth held in common. The more truth we hold in common, the closer will be our fellowship, and vice versa. The same principle applies to the invitation of preachers to speak in our pulpits.

Finally, we consider how full subscriptionism affects the appointment of pastors. The same criteria that pertain to church membership applies to pastors. A prospective pastor who differs on those matters that are regarded by the church as not essential or necessary may be appointed to office with the proviso that he respects the position of the church and do not make an issue of those matters. A pastor who has changed his view on any article of the Confession has the duty to make it known to the eldership of the church. If his new conviction is regarded by the church as contrary to the non-negotiables of the church, he is obliged to resign from office as well as from membership.

The two ordination vows used in many Presbyterian churches ought to be adapted and adopted by Reformed Baptist churches. The first vow is:

"Do you believe the Scriptures of the Old and New Testament, as originally given, to be the inerrant word of God, the infallible rule of faith and practice?"

The second ordination vow is:

"Do you sincerely receive and adopt the 1689 Baptist Confession of Faith as containing the system of doctrine taught in the Holy Scriptures; and do you further promise that if at any time you find yourself out of accord with any of the articles of this system of doctrine, you will on your own initiative, make known to the eldership of this church the change which has taken place in your views since the assumption of this ordination vow?"

4.4 Conclusion

We have covered much ground in this article. Those who are new to the idea of full subscription may think that we are treading on the border of the absurd. But please be clear as to the issue that is at stake. The full subscriptionist holds to the Confession as containing the system of truth taught in the Bible. The loose subscriptionist holds to the system he believes to be biblical, but not specifically defined, which he claims is contained in the Confession. Since that system of doctrine is not specifically defined, he is free to define it for himself. The loose subscriptionist, while professing adherence to the Confession of Faith, actually does not place much value on the Confession. The full subscriptionists may not be in total agreement among themselves on the application of their position to the ministry and life of the church, but they do declare their conviction by holding to the Confession.

Today, we have the problem of non-confessional Calvinists who

49

claim to be Reformed when, strictly speaking, they do not qualify to be called such. We also have the problem of the supposedly confessional churches who do not see the danger or inconsistency of their Loose Subscription position. A truly confessional church will hold to the Full Subscription position.

Those of us who are full subscriptionists must be mindful that correct doctrine alone – without obedience, love, and spiritual vitality – counts for nothing in the end. May God help us to hold to our doctrinal integrity as we subscribe to the Confession of Faith. Amen.

4.5   References

1 Miller, Samuel. 1989. Doctrinal Integrity, Presbyterian Heritage Publications.

2 Smith, Morton H. 1994. The Subscription Debate, Greenville Presbyterian Theological Seminary.

Five

BUILDING UPON THE FOUNDATION

The Reformers and the Puritans were characterised by the spirit of 'semper reformanda' – 'always being reformed'. Sadly, that spirit was lost in the subsequent generations of Christians, who veered away from Scripture in the direction of doctrinal extremes and practical activism. There were those who became hyper-Calvinist, taking the sovereignty of God to the extreme, at the expense of human responsibility. There were others who became Socinians, denying the eternal sonship of Christ, thereby denying the doctrine of the Trinity. Yet others were carried away by enthusiasm in soul-winning in a time of revival but at the expense of doctrinal integrity, leading to ecumenical missions and social concerns. How may we prevent ourselves from straying to such byways in our generation? The answer lies in grasping what are involved in upholding the spirit of 'semper reformanda' while holding firmly to the 1689 Confession. The foundation has been laid by our spiritual forebears – the Reformers, the Puritans, and the framers of the 1689 Confession. We desire to build upon that foundation.

5.1 Word And Spirit

The Holy Spirit inspired chosen men to write down God's word. We are told in 2 Peter 1:21, "...for prophecy never came by the will of man, but holy men of God spoke *as they were* moved by the Holy Spirit." The written word of God is complete, to which nothing is to be added or taken away. The closing words of the Scripture says, in Revelation 22:18-19, "For I testify to everyone who hears the words of the prophecy of this book: If anyone adds to these things, God will add to him the plagues that are written in this book; and if anyone takes away from the words of the book of this prophecy, God shall take away his part from the Book of Life, from the holy city, and from the things which are written in this book." The Scripture has been preserved pure by God's special providence such that it is sufficient for God's people in their walk with Him. We are told, in 2 Timothy 3:16-17, "All Scripture is given by inspiration of God, and is profitable for doctrine, for reproof, for correction, for instruction in righteousness, hat the man of God may be complete, thoroughly equipped for every good work." Scripture is our only authority in all matters of faith and practice.

The Holy Spirit uses the preached word to call out the elect among the hearers into God's kingdom. We are told in Romans 10:17, "...faith comes by hearing, and hearing by the word of God." The believer must "grow in the grace and knowledge of our Lord and Savior Jesus Christ (2 Pet. 3:18)." For this to happen, he must feed on God's word, for "man shall not live by bread alone, but by every word that proceeds from the mouth of God (Matt. 4:4)." The believer must not be content to be "babes in Christ" – like the Corinthian Christians (1 Cor. 3:1). Instead, we are to grow to spiritual maturity. For this to happen, knowledge of, and obedience to, the word of God are essential. We are told in Hebrews 5:13-14, "For everyone who partakes only of milk is unskilled in the word of righteousness, for he is a babe. But solid food belongs to those who are of full age, that is, those who by reason of use have their senses exercised to discern both good and evil."

Moving from the individual to the church, we see again the word of God and the Holy Spirit united in bringing about growth and fruitfulness. We are "...fellow citizens with the saints and members of the household of God, having been built on the foundation of the apostles and prophets, Jesus Christ Himself being the chief cornerstone, in whom the whole building, being fitted together, grows into a holy temple in the Lord (Eph. 2:19-21)." We are assured that God is "...able to do exceedingly abundantly above all that we ask or think, according to the power that works in us (Eph. 3:20)." The local church is "the pillar and ground of the truth (1 Tim. 3:15)" – the pillar to hold high the light of the gospel in a spiritually dark world, and the foundation upon which the faith of believers is built up.

Church leaders play a crucial role in the purposes of God. The spirituality of a church seldom rises above the spirituality of the leaders, and especially of the minister of the word. For the church to be fruitful, the individual members must abide in Christ. The Lord says, in John 15:5, "I am the vine, you are the branches. He who abides in Me, and I in him, bears much fruit; for without Me you can do nothing." Those who abide in Christ will keep His commandments. We are told in 1 John 3:24, "Now he who keeps His commandments abides in Him, and He in him. And by this we know that He abides in us, by the Spirit whom He has given us." Again, the word of God is united to the work of the Holy Spirit in His people. This truth is recognised in the 1689 Confession. In Chapter 1, on the Holy Scriptures, Article 10, we are told,

> The supreme judge, by which all controversies of religion are to be determined, and all decrees of councils, opinions of ancient writers, doctrines of men, and private opinions, are to be examined, and in whose verdict we are to rest, can be no other but the Holy Scripture delivered by the Spirit. In this Scripture so delivered, our faith is finally resolved.

The word of God and the Holy Spirit may not be separated. The spirit of 'semper refomanda' cannot exist in those who do not hold to the primacy of Scripture with dependence on the leading of the Holy Spirit. Christ is most glorified in those who have a passion to uphold and proclaim God's word in the power of the Spirit. It behoves church leaders, and especially the minister of the word, to be filled with the Holy Spirit as they lead the flock and teach the word.

5.2 The Confession Of Faith

When King Solomon built the temple in Jerusalem, he followed closely the design given to King David by divine revelation. As we

53

build the spiritual temple of God today, we will be helped greatly to follow the design given by the written revelation of God. The confessions of faith that arose from the Reformation and the Puritan age may be likened to attempts to discover the design for the temple of God from the Scripture. It took time, effort, discussions, debates, and controversies to arrive at their conclusions. They might not have been right in every detail, but they were right in the main. It would be foolish to reject the confessions of faith to re-invent the wheel. In many new missions situation, there is an aversion for 'denominations' and a desire to be 'indigenous'. The churches end up going through the same struggles over issues that have been encountered by previous generations of Christians in other parts of the world. The solutions they come up with are seldom satisfactory nor scriptural.

Changing the illustration, we might consider the confession of faith as a road map. While it does not provide all the details, nor anticipate all contingencies, it is a helpful guide in our journey to the celestial city. We are not following a road map drawn up by unreliable people, whose foundational premises are questionable. The Reformers had to reject the superstitions and human traditions of the medieval church. Instead, we are following a road map drawn up by men who shared the same commitment to the sole authority of Scripture as we do, and the same desire to glorify God by obedience to His word as we do. The Holy Spirit who works in us today worked in them as well. To the extent that their findings are reliable, to that extent we follow them. On our part, we must allow the word of God to speak to us, and the the Holy Spirit to work in us, today.

The word of God is a living word. The Holy Spirit works in God's people in every generation. While being guided by the confession of faith, we are not fettered by it. After all, it is only a tool – the design, or the road map – in our service to God. We quote more fully the sentiment expressed by the Separatist leader, John Robinson (1575-1625):

> "I charge you before God and His blessed angels, that you follow me no further than you have seen me follow the Lord Jesus Christ. If God reveals anything to you by any instrument of His, be as ready to receive it as you were to receive any truth by my ministry, for I am verily persuaded the Lord hath more truth yet to break forth

out of His Holy word. For my part, I cannot sufficiently bewail the condition of those reformed churches which are come to a period [i.e. a fullstop] in religion, and will go, at present, no further than the instruments of their reformation. The Lutherans cannot be drawn to go beyond what Luther saw; whatever part of His will our God has revealed to Calvin, they will rather die than embrace it; and the Calvinists, you see, stick fast where they were left by that great man of God, who yet saw not all things. This is a misery much to be lamented, for though they were burning and shining lights in their times, yet they penetrated not into the whole counsel of God; but were they now living, would be as willing to embrace further light as that which they first received, for it is not possible the Christian world should come so lately out of such thick anti-christian darkness and that perfection of knowledge should break forth at once."[1]

5.3   Unresolved Issues

Among professing Reformed Baptists today are issues that have not been resolved. These unresolved issues will continue to be a hindrance to the advance of the Reformed Baptist cause and therefore, to that extent, the advance of truth in a needy world. The issues may be considered under the three offices of Christ.

Prophethood

Prophethood has to do with doctrine. There are churches that profess to be Reformed Baptist but have not progressed beyond the Five Points of Calvinism. While declaring adherence to the 1689 Confession, there seems be a lack of appreciation of its content and the practical implications. The Scripture is not preached in a systematic, expository, and applied manner. Deficiency in understanding the doctrines of salvation, sanctification, providence, God's covenant, the church, the Lord's Day, etc. will be reflected in the weaknesses in the life of the members and the church. How, and why, do we differ

---

[1]Broadbent, pp. 245-246.

55

from the General Baptists, the paedobaptists, the charismatics, and the dispensationalists? Why do we reject Contemporary Worship? Why do we value and observe the Lord's Day? How do we relate to other Christians, to the para-church organisations, to missions?

It is possible for any truth of Scripture to be taken to the extreme. In coming out of Arminianism to embrace Calvinism, it is possible for one to swing to hyper-Calvinism. In rejecting the excesses of the Charismatic movement on the 'gifts of the Holy Spirit', it is possible for one to under-emphasise the role of the Holy Spirit in the Christian life. In avoiding the legalism of keeping the Lord's Day seen in some quarters, it is possible for one to fail to uphold the scriptural teaching on the Lord's Day. In emphasising that we are 'Reformed', we might under-emphasise that we are 'Baptist'. The distinctive characteristics of Baptists are not just believer's baptism and the autonomy of the local church but also the voluntary nature of discipleship, the separation of church and state, the practical implications of the three offices of Christ, and mission-mindedness. The liberty of conscience – expressed in the separation of church and state, and in the voluntary nature of discipleship – was championed by the Baptists more than others. Article 10 in Chapter 26 of the 1689 Confession – on the three offices of Christ – was based on the First London Baptist Confession of 1644, Article XIV, and not found in the Westminster Confession. The Particular Baptists were far more mission-minded than any others from the 17th century to the 19th century. The 1689 Confession is, after all, a *Baptist* confession. If the 1689 Confession were better appreciated, taught, and applied a huge difference will be seen in churches that claim to be Reformed Baptist but are stuck at the Five Points of Calvinism.

It is also possible to compromise the teaching of Scripture by mixing truth with error. The sole authority of Scripture is acknowledged at the same time that 'secondary prophecy' of the kind 'not on par with Scripture' is accepted. The Reformed doctrine of salvation (viz. Calvinism) is accepted at the same time that Charismatic style worship (Contemporary worship) is practised. The sovereignty of God in salvation, by the hearing of the preached word, is acknowledged at the same time that the altar-call of Arminianism is practised. If such compromises are due to ignorance, there is the possibility of correction. If they are due to the desire to please men rather than God, there will be not much hope of change. We have no right to dictate to others, but we suggest that it is inappropriate and confusing for such churches to use the name 'Reformed'.

Priesthood

Priesthood has to do with worship. Quite a number of churches that profess to be Reformed Baptist have succumbed to Contemporary Worship – in which is clapping, arm-swaying, the singing of gospel songs, and the use of multiple music instruments. They might not have gone all the way to introduce the drum-set and dancing but there is a clear departure from the worship style of the conservative churches, including the Reformed ones. This occurs in the midst of a subtle undervaluing of the Lord's Day in such churches. There is a failure to appreciate the historic battles fought for the purity of worship and the recovery of the Lord's Day. The clear and strong teaching on worship and the keeping of the Lord's Day in the 1689 Confession is wholly ignored.

The Puritans had to fight the battle on two fronts – the human innovations in worship of the Roman Catholic Church, and the the desecration of the Sabbath by the libertines. John Bunyan describes the snare of Vanity Fair in his book 'Pilgrim's Progress'. Richard Baxter recalled his younger days in an English village, saying,

> "We could not on the Lord's Day either read a chapter, or pray, or sing a psalm, or catechise or instruct a servant, for the noise of the piper and tabor, and shouting in the streets continually in our ears, and we were the common scorn of all rabble in the streets, and we were called Puritans, precisionists, hypocrites because we rather chose on the Lord's day to read the Scriptures rather than what they did."[2]

Today, the advocates of Contemporary Worship have managed to introduce a worldliness in attitude and approach into worship. There is no more reverence for God and the Lord's Day. There is no more solemnity combined with joy in worship. Instead, there is a casualness in attitude and a carelessness in approach – seen even in the casual dressing of the church leaders. Like the proverbial frog

---

[2]Hulse, pp. 135-136.

cooked in increasingly hot water, God's people have become immune to the danger posed by worldliness. We need to awaken to the teaching of Scripture concerning worldliness. We are told in 1 John 2:15, "Do not love the world or the things in the world. If anyone loves the world, the love of the Father is not in him." James 4:4 says, "Adulterers and adulteresses! Do you not know that friendship with the world is enmity with God? Whoever therefore wants to be a friend of the world makes himself an enemy of God."

It is necessary for a confessional Reformed Baptist church to separate from Contemporary Worship.[3] The teaching of 2 Corinthians 6:17-18 applies – "Come out from among them and be separate, says the Lord. Do not touch what is unclean, and I will receive you." "I will be a Father to you, and you shall be My sons and daughters, says the Lord Almighty."

Kingship

Kingship has to do with church government and missions. The Lord, as Head of the church, rules over His people by the word of God. He leads His people into spiritual battles according to the Great Commission (cf. Matt. 28:18-20). Here, our particular concern is with a fault line that has developed between confessional Reformed Baptists over the nature of the eldership and the manner of executing pastoral oversight.

A particular understanding of the eldership – called the Equality View, or Parity View – came into vogue from the 1980s among Calvinist Baptists. Not all these Calvinist Baptists call themselves 'Reformed Baptists', and not all of them hold to the 1689 Confession (some of them hold to the 1646 Confession). We shall confine our discussion to the Reformed Baptists, i.e. those who call themselves such, and claim adherence to the 1689 Confession. Reformed Baptists believe that:

i There are only two offices that continue in the local church since the completion of the written word of God and the passing away of the apostles. The offices are that of elders and deacons. There is no third office of 'minister' which is above the offices of elders and deacons in power.

---

[3]Poh, In Spirit and Truth.

ii The elders are the ones who exercise rule over the church. The deacons do not rule but take care of the mundane affairs of the church, under the oversight of the elders. The qualifications for the offices of elders and deacons are as taught in 1 Timothy 3:1-13 and related passages.

iii The church should be ruled by an eldership, made up of a plurality of elders. In unusual circumstances a church may have no elder, or only one elder, in which case it should place itself under the oversight of an established church.

iv The office of elder is one and the same as the office of bishop. The words 'elder' and 'bishop' are used interchangeably in the Scripture. The idea of a 'bishop' who rules over many congregations cannot be convincingly supported from Scripture.

The commonality ends here. The differences among the Reformed Baptists over the eldership may be contrasted under what I would call the Traditional View and the Parity View. (See Fig. 5.1.) The Traditional View corresponds to the view of eldership found in the Independent form of church government practised by the Particular Baptists and the Congregationalists of the 17th century.

I have shown at length elsewhere that the Traditional View is scriptural.[4] In 1 Timothy 5:17, we are told, "Let the elders who rule well be counted worthy of double honor, especially those who labor in the word and doctrine." The attempt by the advocates of the Parity View to dilute the force of the word 'especially' (Greek, *malista*) has been unconvincing. In Ephesians 4:11, we are told, "And He Himself gave some to be apostles, some prophets, some evangelists, and some pastors and teachers..." Exegetically, 'pastors and teachers' is one office. Although an ordinary office, it is mentioned together with the extraordinary offices because, as shown by the context, the proclamation of God's word is in view. The primacy of God's word is everywhere upheld in the Scripture. It is, therefore, right to draw the conclusion that the call of God is needed for this awesome task. The elders who 'labor in word and doctrine' (1 Tim. 5:17) are called 'pastors and teachers' here. The pastors are the regular teachers of God's word in the church. The noun 'pastors' is used, unlike the verb 'to shepherd' in Acts 20:28, which says, "Therefore take heed to yourselves and to all the flock, among which the Holy Spirit has

Traditional View	Parity View
There are two types of elders — teaching elders and ruling elders.	The elders are not divided into two types but they differ from one another in gifts.
All pastors are elders, but not all elders are pastors. The teaching elder (usually one in each church) is called the pastor.	All elders are pastors, and all pastors are elders.
The pastor has a special calling from God to handle the word full-time, in addition to possessing the qualifications of an elder.	There is no special calling to preach God's word, unlike the extraordinary officers of prophets and apostles. The elder who is gifted is supported full-time to preach regularly.

Fig. 5.1 Traditional and Parity Views of the Eldership

made you overseers, to shepherd the church of God which He purchased with His own blood." All elders shepherd the church of God, but not all elders are called and set apart full-time as pastors, to teach God's word on a regular basis.

I have also shown elsewhere that the Traditional View was held by the Particular Baptists in the 17th century, up to the time when the Second London Baptist Confession of Faith was affirmed in 1689.[5] Up to that time, a high view of the ministry was upheld by the Puritans, as required by Scripture. Benjamin Keach, and his son Elias, were about the only Particular Baptists known to have advocated the Parity View. The problems that arose from that view in subsequent years, starting from the time of Benjamin Keach, are reappearing today, with new ones added in. What are some of those problems?

Firstly, the traditional Reformed doctrine of the call to the ministry of the word – as taught by men such as C. H. Spurgeon, John Newton, and Charles Bridges – is denied or differently understood. This will have the long-term effect of undermining the ministry of

---

[4]Poh, The Keys of the Kingdom.
[5]Poh, A Garden Enclosed.

the word. An early and strong proponent of the Equality (his own term) View taught a clear doctrine of the call to the ministry which stood in such obvious contradiction to his idea of the equality of all elders.[6] Today, the doctrine of the call to the ministry is rejected by other advocates. By denying the doctrine of the call, there will be a lowering of the quality of the ministry of the word as uncalled men are appointed to preach – either full-time as the regular preachers, or in rotation as lay-preachers, as practised among the Plymouth Brethren. In a situation where there is a full-time pastor who dies or is removed for whatever reason, one of the remaining 'pastors' will naturally take over the role of full-time preacher. The ministry is only a task to be carried out, not a calling from God.

Secondly, the constant attempt of the elders to defer to one another due to the belief in equality has resulted in the reinforcement of any judgement made by the eldership against the perceived wrong done by a member of the church, with devastating consequences. Members of the church are also subjected to close pastoral oversight that intrudes into personal and family liberties because all elders are pastors who must shepherd the flock. This particular style of pastoral oversight has been called 'heavy shepherding'. We hasten to add that not all churches that adopt the Parity View are guilty of heavy shepherding. Furthermore, heavy shepherding is not confined to only churches that hold to the Parity View. However, the great tendency towards heavy shepherding among such churches has been seen since the rise of the Parity View in the 1980s.

Thirdly, there are some men who, while professing to hold to the Parity View as well as the traditional Reformed understanding of the call to the ministry, hesitate or are reluctant to appoint another 'co-pastor' to make up a plurality of elders. They sense the impracticality of having two, or more, called men to be in the same church. The outcome is that there is no eldership to speak of in their churches while they wait for "the right time" for at least one co-pastor to be appointed. This was the dilemma faced by the early advocates of the Parity View like Benjamin Keach (1640-1704) and John Gill (1697-1771). By denying the role of 'ruling elders' while not having another 'co-pastor', the Parity View had contributed in no small measure to the system of one-pastor-many-deacons prevail-

---

[6]Martin. Prepared to Preach.

ing in later Particular Baptist churches. When there are two equally called ministers in the church, the ministry of the word is effectively halved for each man. The ministers will not be content to be underused. Tension is bound to arise between the two men, leading to a parting of ways.

The question may be asked, which view of the eldership is taught in the 1689 Confession – the Parity View or the Traditional View? The advocates of the Parity View have attempted to imposed their view upon the Confession while those who hold to the Traditional View have continued to claim that their view is taught in the Confession. Of the thirty-seven signatories to the Confession in 1689, the only person clearly known to have held to the Parity View was Benjamin Keach. The terms 'Parity View' and 'Traditional View' are anachronistic, introduced for convenience. The vast majority of the Particular Baptists are known to have held to the Traditional View of eldership, different from that of Benjamin Keach. Keach, who was from the General Baptist background, and continued to have close interaction with the General Baptists despite turning Calvinist, was known to be a controversial character. He would have agitated for the Confession to be worded to his taste. However, the majority of the men present would not have allowed it to be changed to the extent that their view was not reflected in the document. Let us consider the Confession. (The reader might want to refer to it in the second part of this book.)

Chapter 26 of the Confession, entitled "Of The Church", was taken wholly from the Platform of Church Polity, appended to the 'Savoy Declaration of Faith and Order' of the Congregationalists. Only minor amendments were made since the Particular Baptists basically held to the same form of church government as the Congregationalists. Indeed, the Particular Baptists had originated from the Congregationalists, differing from them only on the sprinkling and membership of infants born to believers. Chapter 26, Article 8 of the 1689 Confession shows that only two offices abide in the church – the offices of elders and deacons. Articles 8 and 9 reveal that the words 'elders' and 'bishops' are interchangeable. Article 10 uses the word 'pastor' for those who are supported full-time in the ministry of the word. Article 11 shows that the pastor is also a bishop, or elder. The elders have the responsibility over the teaching ministry of the church but others who are gifted and approved by the church may be called upon to preach as well. This straightforward understanding of the Confession's teaching on the eldership is consistent with the Traditional View, known to be held by the Particular Baptists. We have shown that it is also consistent with the teaching of Scripture.

The Confession teaches that all pastors are elders, but not all elders are pastors. Further confirmation is found in Chapter 28 of the Confession, "Of Baptism and the Lord's Supper". In Article 2, we are told, "These holy appointments are to be administered by those only who are qualified and called to it, according to the commission of Christ." These words are strong and unambiguous. Only those who are qualified and called, and that according to the commission of Christ, may administer baptism and the Lord's Supper. The administration of these special ordinances may be delegated to others but the authority to administer them remains with the minister of the gospel. The administration of these special ordinances are, after all, the public and visible proclamation of the gospel. The scripture references for this article of the Confession are Matthew 28:19 and 1 Corinthians 4:1, both of which concern those set apart to preach God's word.

Another confirmation is found in Chapter 30, "Of The Lord's Supper". In Article 3, we are told, "The Lord Jesus has, in this ordinance, appointed His ministers to pray and bless the elements of bread and wine – and so setting them apart from a common to a holy use – and to take and break the bread, then to take the cup, and they partaking also themselves, to give both to the partakers." Christ's ministers are those who have a calling from God and set apart full-time to preach God's word. The Puritans, who included the Particular Baptists, understood and used the word 'ministers' in this sense. Some ministers worked part-time when they could not be supported fully by the church, but the aim was always for them to be supported fully.

We have discussed the difference over the eldership between confessional Reformed Baptists at some length to prove that the Traditional View is taught in the 1689 Confession. Our hearts long for greater agreement and unity among the Reformed Baptists. The fault line between advocates of the two views has become increasingly wide. This has caused disquiet in some quarters, what with the charge of heavy-shepherding levelled at the Reformed Baptists – rightly or wrongly. If the advocates of the the Parity View are not open to reconsider their position, we suggest that they amend the Confession by adding a separate chapter to more clearly reflect their view, and calling it by a different name – as was done with the Philadelphia Confession.

5.4   Conclusion

The unresolved issues among the Reformed Baptists might cause the uninitiated to despair over the situation and loose heart over associating with them. When the Lord Jesus asked His disciples, "Do you also want to go away?" Simon Peter answered, saying, "Lord, to whom shall we go? You have the words of eternal life. Also we have come to believe and know that You are the Christ, the Son of the living God (John 6:67-69)." Just as we do not want to turn away from the Lord, we do not want to turn away from His word. The 1689 Confession is an accurate, albeit imperfect, expression of that word. It is worthy of our love, our respect, and our propagation of it.

5.5   References

1 Broadbent, E. H. 1981. The Pilgrim Church, Picketing & Inglis.

2 Hulse, Erroll. 2000. Who Are The Puritans? Evangelical Press

3 Martin, A. N. 1981. Prepared to Preach, Covenanter Press.

4 Poh, B. S. 2017. The Keys of the Kingdom, Good News Enterprise.

5 Poh, B. S. 2016. A Garden Enclosed, Good News Enterprise.

6 Poh, B. S. 2020. In Spirit and Truth, Good News Enterprise.

✳ ✳ ✳ ✳ ✳

THE 1689 CONFESSION

The 1689 Confession: Contents

✳ ✳ ✳ ✳ ✳

1. The Holy Scriptures

1 The Holy Scripture is the only sufficient, certain, and infallible rule of all saving knowledge, faith, and obedience,[1] although the light of nature, and the works of creation and providence do so far manifest the goodness, wisdom, and power of God, as to leave men inexcusable. However, they are not sufficient to give that knowledge of God and His will which is necessary to salvation.[2] Therefore it pleased the Lord at sundry times and in divers manners to reveal Himself, and to declare His will to His church.[3] Afterward, for the better preserving and propagating of the truth, and for the more sure establishment and comfort of the church against the corruption of the flesh, and the malice of Satan, and of the world, He committed it wholly to writing, which makes the Holy Scriptures to be most necessary, those former ways of God's revealing His will to His people being now ceased.[4]

[1]2 Tim. 3:15-17; Isa. 8:20; Luke 16:29, 31; Eph. 2:20. [2]Rom. 1:19-21; 2:14-15; Ps. 19:1-3. [3]Heb. 1:1. [4]Prov. 22:19-21; Rom. 15:4; 2 Pet. 1:19-20.

2 Under the name of Holy Scripture, or the word of God written, are now contained all the books of the Old and New Testament, which are these:

OF THE OLD TESTAMENT			
Genesis	1 Kings	Ecclesiastes	Amos
Exodus	2 Kings	The Song of	Obadiah
Leviticus	1 Chronicles	Solomon	Jonah
Numbers	2 Chronicles	Isaiah	Micah
Deuteronomy	Ezra	Jeremiah	Nahum
Joshua	Nehemiah	Lamentations	Habakkuk
Judges	Esther	Ezekiel	Zephaniah
Ruth	Job	Daniel	Haggai
1 Samuel	Psalms	Hosea	Zechariah
2 Samuel	Proverbs	Joel	Malachi

OF THE NEW TESTAMENT			
Matthew	1 Corinthians	2 Thessalonians	1 Peter
Mark	2 Corinthians	1 Timothy	2 Peter
Luke	Galatians	2 Timothy	1 John
John	Ephesians	Titus	2 John
The Acts of	Philippians	Philemon	3 John
the Apostles	Colossians	Hebrews	Jude
Romans	1 Thessalonians	James	Revelation

All of which are given by the inspiration of God, to be the rule of faith and life.[5]

[5] 2 Tim. 3:16.

3 The books commonly called Apocrypha, not being of divine inspiration, are no part of the canon or rule of the Scripture, and, therefore, are of no authority to the church of God, nor to be in any way approved or made use of than other human writings.[6]

[6] Luke 24:27, 44; Rom. 3:2.

4 The authority of the Holy Scripture, for which it ought to be believed, depends not upon the testimony of any man or church, but

wholly upon God (who is Truth itself), the Author. Therefore it is to be received because it is the word of God.[7]

[7]2 Peter 1:19-21; 2 Tim. 3:16; 2 Thess. 2:13; 1 John 5:9.

5 We may be moved and induced by the testimony of the church of God to a high and reverent esteem of the Holy Scriptures, and the heavenliness of the matter – the efficacy of the doctrine, and the majesty of the style, the agreement of all the parts, the scope of the whole (which is to give all glory to God), the full discovery it makes of the only way of man's salvation, and many other incomparable excellencies, and entire perfections – are arguments whereby it does abundantly evidence itself to be the word of God. Despite these, our full persuasion and assurance of the infallible truth, and its divine authority, is from the inward work of the Holy Spirit bearing witness by and with the word in our hearts.[8]

[8]John 16:13, 14; 1 Cor. 2:10-12; 1 John 2:20, 27.

6 The whole counsel of God concerning all things necessary for His own glory, man's salvation, faith and life, is either expressly set down or necessarily contained in the Holy Scripture, to which nothing at any time is to be added, whether by new revelation of the Spirit, or traditions of men.[9] Nevertheless, we acknowledge the inward illumination of the Spirit of God to be necessary for the saving understanding of such things as are revealed in the word,[10] and that there are some circumstances concerning the worship of God, and government of the church, common to human actions and societies, which are to be ordered by the light of nature and Christian prudence, according to the general rules of the word, which are always to be observed.[11]

[9]2 Tim. 3:15-17; Gal. 1:8, 9. [10]John 4:45; 1 Cor. 2:9-12. [11]1 Cor. 11:13, 14; 14:26, 40.

7 All things in Scripture are not alike plain in themselves, nor alike clear to all,[12] yet those things which are necessary to be known, believed and observed for salvation, are so clearly propounded and opened in some place of Scripture or other, that not only the learned, but the unlearned, in a due use of ordinary means, may attain to a sufficient understanding of them.[13]

[12]2 Pet. 3:16. [13]Ps. 19:7; 119:130.

8 The Old Testament in Hebrew (which was the native language of the people of God of old),[14] and the New Testament in Greek (which at the time of the writing of it was most generally known to the nations), being immediately inspired by God, and by His singular care and providence kept pure in all ages, are therefore authentic, so that in all controversies of religion, the church is finally to appeal to them.[15] But because these original tongues are not known to all the people of God who have a right unto, and interest in, the Scriptures, and are commanded in the fear of God to read[16] and search them,[17] therefore they are to be translated into the common language of every nation to which they come.[18] In that way, the word of God dwells plentifully in all, that they may worship Him in an acceptable manner, and through patience and comfort of the Scriptures may have hope.[19]

[14]Rom. 3:2. [15]Isa. 8:20. [16]Acts 15:15. [17]John 5:39. [18]1 Cor. 14:6, 9, 11, 12, 24, 28. [19]Col. 3:16.

9 The infallible rule of interpretation of Scripture is the Scripture itself, and therefore when there is a question about the true and full sense of any Scripture (which is not manifold, but one), it must be searched by other places that speak more clearly.[20]

[20]2 Pet. 1:20, 21; Acts 15:15, 16.

10 The supreme judge, by which all controversies of religion are to be determined, and all decrees of councils, opinions of ancient writers, doctrines of men, and private opinions, are to be examined, and in whose verdict we are to rest, can be no other but the Holy Scripture delivered by the Spirit. In this Scripture so delivered, our faith is finally resolved.[21]

[21]Matt. 22:29, 31, 32; Eph. 2:20; Acts 28:23.

2. God And The Holy Trinity

1 The Lord our God is but one only living and true God;[1] whose subsistence is in and of Himself,[2] infinite in being and perfection; whose essence cannot be comprehended by any but Himself;[3] a most pure spirit,[4] invisible, without body, parts, or passions, who only has immortality, dwelling in the light which no man can approach unto;[5] who is immutable,[6] immense,[7] eternal,[8] incomprehensible, almighty,[9] every way infinite, most holy,[10] most wise, most free, most absolute; working all things according to the counsel of His own immutable and most righteous wills[11] for His own glory;[12] most loving gracious, merciful, long-suffering, abundant in goodness and truth, forgiving iniquity, transgression, and sin; the rewarder of them that diligently seek Him,[13] and furthermore most just and terrible in His judgments,[14] hating all sin,[15] and who will by no means clear the guilty.[16]

[1]1 Cor. 8:4, 6; Deut. 6:4. [2]Jer. 10:10; Isa. 98:12. [3]Exod. 3:14. [4]John 4:24. [5]1 Tim. 1:17; Deut. 4:15-16. [6]Mal. 3:6. [7]1 Kings 8:27; Jer. 23:23. [8]Ps. 90:2. [9]Gen. 17:1. [10]Isa. 6:3. [11]Ps. 115:3; Isa. 46:10. [12]Prov. 16:4; Rom. 11:36. [13]Exod. 34:6, 7; Heb. 11:6. [14]Neh. 9:32-33. [15]Ps. 5:5-6. [16]Exod. 34:7; Nahum 1:2-3.

2 God, having all life,[17] glory,[18] goodness,[19] blessedness, in and of Himself, is alone in and unto Himself all-sufficient, not standing in need of any creature which He has made, nor deriving any glory from them,[20] but only manifesting His own glory in, by, unto, and upon them. He is the alone fountain of all being, of whom, through whom, and to whom are all things,[21] and He has most sovereign dominion over all creatures, to do by them, for them, or upon them, whatsoever Himself pleases.[22] In His sight all things

are open and manifest,[23] His knowledge is infinite, infallible, and independent upon the creature, so as nothing is to Him contingent or uncertain.[24] He is most holy in all His counsels, in all His works,[25] and in all His commands. To Him is due from angels and men, all worship,[26] service, or obedience – which as creatures they owe unto the Creator – and whatever He is further pleased to require of them.

[17]John 5:26. [18]Ps. 148:13. [19]Ps. 119:68. [20]Job 22:2-3. [21]Rom. 11:34-36. [22]Dan. 4:25, 34-35. [23]Heb. 4:13. [24]Ezek. 11:5, Acts 15:18. [25]Ps. 145:17. [26]Rev. 5:12-14.

3 In this divine and infinite Being there are three subsistences – the Father, the Word or Son, and Holy Spirit[27] – of one substance, power, and eternity, each having the whole divine essence, yet the essence undivided.[28] The Father is of none, neither begotten nor proceeding; the Son is eternally begotten of the Father;[29] the Holy Spirit proceeding from the Father and the Son;[30] all infinite, without beginning, therefore but one God, who is not to be divided in nature and being, but distinguished by several special relative properties and personal relations; which doctrine of the Trinity is the foundation of all our communion with God, and comfortable dependence on Him.

[27]1 John 5:7; Matt. 28:19, 2 Cor. 13:14. [28]Exod. 3:14, John 14:11, 1 Cor. 8:6. [29]John 1:14, 18. [30]John 15:26. Gal. 4:6.

3. God's Decree

1 God has decreed in Himself, from all eternity, by the most wise and holy counsel of His own will, freely and unchangeably, all things, whatsoever comes to pass;[1] yet so as that God is neither the author of sin nor has fellowship with any of it.[2] Nor is force placed on the will of the creature, nor yet is the liberty or contingency of second causes taken away, but rather established,[3] in which appears His wisdom in disposing all things, and power and faithfulness in accomplishing His decree.[4]

[1]Isa. 46:10; Eph. 1:11; Heb. 6:17; Rom. 9:15, 18. [2]James 1:13; 1 John 1:5. [3]Acts 4:27-28; John 19:11. [4]Num. 23:19; Eph. 1:3-5.

2 Although God knows whatever may or can come to pass, upon all supposed conditions,[5] yet He has not decreed anything because He foresaw it as in the future, or as that which would come to pass upon such conditions.[6]

[5]Acts 15:18. [6]Rom. 9:11, 13, 16, 18.

3 By the decree of God, for the manifestation of His glory, some men and angels are predestinated, or foreordained to eternal life through Jesus Christ,[7] to the praise of His glorious grace.[8] Others are left to act in their sin to their just condemnation, to the praise of His glorious justice.[9]

[7]1 Tim. 5:21; Matt. 25:34. [8]Eph. 1:5-6. [9]Rom. 9:22-23; Jude 4.

4 These angels and men thus predestined and foreordained, are particularly and unchangeably designed, and their number so certain and definite, that it cannot be either increased or diminished.[10]

[10]2 Tim. 2:19; John 13:18.

5 Those of mankind that are predestined to life, God, before the foundation of the world was laid, according to His eternal and immutable purpose, and the secret counsel and good pleasure of His will, has chosen in Christ unto everlasting glory, out of His mere free grace and love,[11] without any other thing in the creature as a condition or cause moving Him to do so.[12]

[11]Eph. 1:4, 9, 11; Rom. 8:30; 2 Tim. 1:9; 1 Thess. 5:9. [12]Rom. 9:13, 16; Eph. 2:5, 12.

6 As God has appointed the elect unto glory, so He has, by the eternal and most free purpose of His will, foreordained all the means for it.[13] Accordingly, they who are elected, being fallen in Adam, are redeemed by Christ,[14] are effectually called unto faith in Christ, by His Spirit working in due season, are justified, adopted, sanctified,[15] and kept by His power through faith unto salvation.[16] Neither are any other redeemed by Christ, or effectually called, justified, adopted, sanctified, and saved, but the elect only.[17]

[13]1 Pet. 1:2; 2 Thess. 2:13. [14]1 Thess. 5:9-10. [15]Rom. 8:30; 2 Thess. 2:13. [16]1 Pet. 1:5. [17]John 10:26; 17:9; 6:64.

7 The doctrine of this high mystery of predestination is to be handled with special prudence and care, that men attending the will of God revealed in His word, and yielding obedience to it, may, from the certainty of their effectual vocation, be assured of their eternal election .[18] So shall this doctrine provide cause for praise,[19] reverence, and admiration of God, and of humility,[20] diligence, and abundant consolation to all that sincerely obey the gospel.[21]

[1]1 Thess. 1:4-5; 2 Pet. 1:10. [1]Eph. 1:6; Rom. 11:33. [1]Rom. 11:5-6, 20. [1]Luke 10:20.

4. Creation

1 In the beginning it pleased God the Father, Son, and Holy Spirit,[1] for the manifestation of the glory of His eternal power,[2] wisdom, and goodness, to create or make the world, and all things in it, whether visible or invisible, in the space of six days, and all very good.[3]

[1]John 1:2-3; Heb. 1:2; Job 26:13. [2]Rom. 1:20. [1]Col. 1:16; Gen. 1:31.

2 After God had made all other creatures, He created man, male and female,[4] with rational and immortal souls,[5] rendering them fit unto that life to God for which they were created. They were made after the image of God, in knowledge, righteousness, and true holiness;[6] having the law of God written in their hearts,[7] and power to fulfil it, and yet under a possibility of transgressing, being left to the liberty of their own will, which was subject to change.[8]

[4]Gen. 1:27. [5]Gen. 2:7. [6]Eccl. 7:29; Gen. 1:26. [7]Rom. 2:14-15. [8]Gen. 3:6.

3 Besides the law written in their hearts, they received a command not to eat of the tree of knowledge of good and evil,[9] which whilst they kept, they were happy in their communion with God, and had dominion over the creatures.[10]

[9]Gen. 2:17. [10]Gen. 1:26, 28.

77

5. Divine Providence

1 God the good Creator of all things, in His infinite power and wisdom, does uphold, direct, dispose, and govern all creatures and things,[1] from the greatest even to the least,[2] by His most wise and holy providence. This is to the end for which they were created, according to His infallible foreknowledge, and the free and immutable counsel of His own will – which is, to the praise of the glory of His wisdom, power, justice, infinite goodness, and mercy.[3]

[1]Heb. 1:3; Job 38:11; Isa. 44:10-11; Ps. 135:6. [2]Matt. 10:29-31. [3]Eph. 1:11.

2 Although in relation to the foreknowledge and decree of God, the first cause, all things come to pass immutably and infallibly,[4] so that there is not anything befalls any by chance, or without His providence.[5] Yet by the same providence He orders them to fall out according to the nature of second causes, either necessarily, freely, or contingently.[6]

[4]Acts 2:23. [5]Prov. 16:33. [6]Gen. 8:22.

3 God, in His ordinary providence makes use of means,[7] yet is free to work without,[8] above,[9] and against them[10] at His pleasure.

[7]Acts 27:31, 44; Isa. 55:10, 11. [8]Hos. 1:7. [9]9Rom. 4:19-21. [10]Dan. 3:27.

4 The almighty power, unsearchable wisdom, and infinite goodness of God, so far manifest themselves in His providence, that His determinate counsel extends itself even to the first fall, and all other sinful actions both of angels and men.[11] That happens not by a bare permission, but which also He most wisely and powerfully

bounds, and otherwise orders and governs,[12] in a manifold management to His most holy ends.[13] Yet so, the sinfulness of their acts proceeds only from the creatures, and not from God, who, being most holy and righteous, neither is nor can be the author or approver of sin.[14]

[11]Rom. 11:32-34; 2 Sam. 24:1; 1 Chron. 21:1. [12]2 Kings 19:28, Ps. 76:10. [13]Gen. 50:20; Isa. 10:6, 7, 12. [14]Ps. 50:21; 1 John 2:16.

5 The most wise, righteous, and gracious God does oftentimes leave for a season His own children to manifold temptations and the corruptions of their own hearts, to chastise them for their former sins, or to reveal to them the hidden strength of corruption and deceitfulness of their hearts, that they may be humbled. It is also to raise them to a more close and constant dependence for their support upon Himself; and to make them more watchful against all future occasions of sin, and for other just and holy ends.[15] So that whatever befalls any of His elect is by His appointment, for His glory, and their good.[16]

[15]2 Chron. 32:25-26, 31; 2 Cor. 12:7-9. [16]Rom. 8:28.

6 As for those wicked and ungodly men whom God, as a righteous judge, for former sin does blind and harden;[17] from them He not only withholds His grace, whereby they might have been enlightened in their understanding, and work upon their hearts;[18] but sometimes also withdraws the gifts which they had,[19] and exposes them to such objects as their corruption makes occasion of sin.[20] Furthermore, God gives them over to their own lusts, the temptations of the world, and the power of Satan,[21] whereby it comes to pass that they harden themselves, under those means which God uses for the softening of others.[22] [17]Rom. 1:24-26, 28; 11:7-8.

[18]Deut. 29:4. [19]Matt. 13:12. [20]Deut. 2:30; 2 Kings 8:12-13. [21]Ps. 81:11-12; 2 Thess. 2:10-12. [22]Exod. 8:15, 32; Isa. 6:9-10; 1 Pet. 2:7-8.

7 As the providence of God does in general reach to all creatures, so after a more special manner it takes care of His church, and

disposes all things to her good.[23]

[23] 1 Tim. 4:10; Amos 9:8-9; Isa. 43:3-5.

6. The Fall, Sin, Punishment

1 Although God created man upright and perfect, and gave him a righteous law, which would have led to life had he kept it, and threatened death upon the breach thereof,[1] yet he did not long abide in this honour. Satan using the subtlety of the serpent to subdue Eve, then by her seducing Adam, who, without any compulsion, did wilfully transgress the law of their creation, and the command given unto them, in eating the forbidden fruit,[2] which God was pleased, according to His wise and holy counsel to permit, having purposed to order it to His own glory.

[1]Gen. 2:16-17. [2]2Gen. 3:12-13, 2 Cor. 11:3.

2 Our first parents, by this sin, fell from their original righteousness and communion with God, and we in them whereby death came upon all.[3] All persons became dead in sin,[4] and wholly defiled in all the faculties and parts of soul and body.[5]

[3]Rom. 3:23. [4]Rom. 5:12, etc. [5]Tit. 1:15; Gen. 6:5; Jer. 17:9; Rom. 3:10-19.

3 They were the root, and by God's appointment, stood in the room and stead of all mankind, so that the guilt of the sin was imputed, and corrupted nature conveyed, to all their posterity descending from them by ordinary generation.[6] They are now conceived in sin,[7] and by nature children of wrath,[8] the servants of sin, the subjects of death,[9] and all other miseries – spiritual, temporal, and eternal – unless the Lord Jesus set them free.[10]

[6]Rom. 5:12-19; 1 Cor. 15:21-22, 45, 49. [7]Ps. 51:5; Job 14:4. [8]Eph. 2:3. [9]Rom. 6:20; 5:12. [10]Heb. 2:14-15; 1 Thess. 1:10.

4 From this original corruption, whereby we are utterly indisposed, disabled, and made opposite to all good, and wholly inclined to all evil,[11] do proceed all actual transgressions.[12]

[11]Rom. 8:7; Col. 1:21. [12]James 1:14-15; Matt. 15:19.

5 The corruption of nature, during this life, does remain in those who are regenerated.[13] Although it is through Christ pardoned and mortified, yet both itself, and its immediate actions, are truly and properly sin.[14]

[13]Rom. 7:18, 23; Eccles. 7:20; 1 John 1:8. [14]Rom. 7:23-25; Gal. 5:17.

7. God's Covenant

1 The distance between God and the creature is so great, that although rational creatures do owe obedience unto Him as their creator, yet they could never have attained the reward of life but by some voluntary condescension on God's part, which He has been pleased to express by way of covenant.[1]

[1]Luke 17:10; Job 35:7-8.

2 Moreover, man having brought himself under the curse of the law by his fall, it pleased the Lord to make a covenant of grace,[2] in which He freely offers to sinners life and salvation by Jesus Christ, requiring of them faith in Him, that they may be saved;[3] and promising to give to all those that are ordained to eternal life, His Holy Spirit, to make them willing and able to believe.[4]

[2]Gen. 2:17; Gal. 3:10; Rom. 3:20-21. [3]Rom. 8:3; Mark 16:15-16; John 3:16. [4]Ezek. 36:26-27; John 6:44-45; Ps. 110:3.

3 This covenant is revealed in the gospel; first of all to Adam in the promise of salvation by the seed of the woman,[5] and afterwards by farther steps, until its full revelation was completed in the New Testament.[6] It is founded in that eternal covenant transaction that was between the Father and the Son about the redemption of the elect.[7] It is by the grace of this covenant alone that all of the posterity of fallen Adam that ever were saved did obtain life and blessed immortality, man being now utterly incapable of acceptance with God upon those terms on which Adam stood in his state of innocency.[8]

[5]Gen. 3:15. [6]Heb. 1:1. [7]2 Tim. 1:9; Tit. 1:2. [8]Heb. 11:6, 13; Rom. 4:1-2, etc.; Acts 4:12; John 8:56.

✳ ✳ ✳ ✳ ✳

8. Christ The Mediator

1 It pleased God, in His eternal purpose, to choose and ordain the Lord Jesus, His only begotten Son, according to the covenant made between them both, to be the Mediator between God and man;[1] – the Prophet,[2] Priest,[3] and King;[4] Head and Saviour of His church,[5] the heir of all things,[6] and Judge of the world;[7] – unto whom He did from all eternity give a people to be His seed and to be by Him in time redeemed, called, justified, sanctified, and glorified.[8]

[1]Isa. 42:1; 1 Pet. 1:19, 20. [2]Acts 3:22. [3]Heb. 5:5-6. [4]Ps. 2:6; Luke 1:33. [5]Eph. 1:22-23. [6]Heb. 1:2. [7]Acts 17:31. [8]Isa. 53:10; John 17:6; Rom. 8:30.

2 The Son of God, the second person in the Holy Trinity, being true and eternal God, the brightness of the Father's glory, of one substance and equal with Him who made the world, who upholds and governs all things He has made, did, when the fulness of time had arrived, take upon Him man's nature, with all the associated essential properties and common infirmities,[9] yet without sin.[10] He was conceived by the Holy Spirit in the womb of the Virgin Mary, the Holy Spirit coming down upon her. The power of the Most High overshadowed her, and so He was made of a woman of the tribe of Judah, of the seed of Abraham and David according to the scriptures.[11] So, two whole, perfect, and distinct natures were inseparably joined together in one person, without conversion, composition, or confusion; which person is truly God and truly man, yet one Christ, the only Mediator between God and man.[12]

⁹John 1:14; Gal. 4:4. ¹⁰Rom. 8:3; Heb. 2:14, 16, 17; 4:15.
¹¹Matt. 1:22-23; Luke 1:27, 31, 35. ¹²Rom. 9:5, 1 Tim. 2:5.

3　The Lord Jesus, in His human nature thus united to the divine,
in the person of the Son, was sanctified and anointed with the
Holy Spirit above measure,[13] having in Him all the treasures of
wisdom and knowledge.[14] In Him it pleased the Father that all
fulness should dwell,[15] to the end that being holy, harmless, un-
defiled,[16] and full of grace and truth,[17] He might be thoroughly
furnished to execute the office of a Mediator and surety.[18] This office He took not upon Himself, but was called to it by His Father;[19]
who also put all power and judgment in His hand, and gave Him
commandment to execute it.[20]

¹³Ps. 45:7; Acts 10:38; John 3:34. ¹⁴Col. 2:3. ¹⁵Col. 1:19. ¹⁶Heb.
7:26. ¹⁷John 1:14. ¹⁸Heb. 7:22. ¹⁹Heb. 5:5. ²⁰John 5:22, 27;
Matt. 28:18; Acts 2:36.

4　This office the Lord Jesus did most willingly undertake,[21] and in
order that He might discharge it He was made under the law.[22]
He did perfectly fulfil it, and underwent the punishment due to us,
which we should have borne and suffered.[23] He was made sin and
a curse for us;[24] enduring most grievous sorrows in His soul, and
most painful sufferings in His body;[25] was crucified, and died, and
remained in the state of the dead, yet saw no corruption.[26] On the
third day He arose from the dead[27] with the same body in which
he suffered,[28] with which He also ascended into heaven,[29] and
there sits at the right hand of His Father making intercession,[30]
and shall return to judge men and angels at the end of the world.[31]

²¹Ps. 40:7, 8; Heb. 10:5-10; John 10:18. ²²Gal. 4:4; Matt. 3:15.
²³Gal. 3:13; Isa. 53:6; 1 Pet. 3:18. ²⁴2 Cor. 5:21. ²⁵Matt. 26:37-
38; Luke 22:44; Matt. 27:46. ²⁶Acts 13:37. ²⁷1 Cor. 15:3-4.
²⁸John 20:25, 27. ²⁹Mark 16:19; Acts 1:9-11. ³⁰Rom. 8:34; Heb.
9:24. ³¹Acts 10:42; Rom. 14:9-10; Acts 1:11; 2 Pet. 2:4.

5　The Lord Jesus, by His perfect obedience and sacrifice of Himself,
which He through the eternal Spirit once offered up unto God, has
fully satisfied the justice of God,[32] procured reconciliation, and
purchased an everlasting inheritance in the kingdom of heaven
for all those whom the Father has given unto Him.[33]

[32]Heb. 9:14; 10:14; Rom. 3:25-26. [33]John 17:2; Heb. 9:15.

6 Although the price of redemption was not actually paid by Christ till after His incarnation, yet the virtue, efficacy, and benefit from it were communicated to the elect in all ages successively from the beginning of the world. This was done in and by those promises, types, and sacrifices wherein He was revealed, and signified to be the seed which should bruise the serpent's head;[34] and the Lamb slain from the foundation of the world,[35] being the same yesterday, and today, and for ever.[36]

[34]1 Cor. 10:4; Heb. 4:2; 1 Pet. 1:10-11. [35]Rev. 13:8. [36]Heb. 13:8.

7 Christ, in the work of mediation, acts according to both natures, by each nature doing that which is proper to itself. Yet by reason of the unity of the person, that which is proper to one nature is sometimes in scripture, attributed to the person mentioned by the other nature.[37]

[37]John 3:13; Acts 20:28.

8 To all those for whom Christ has obtained eternal redemption, He does certainly and effectually apply and communicate it – making intercession for them;[38] uniting them to Himself by His Spirit; revealing to them, in and by the word, the mystery of salvation; persuading them to believe and obey;[39] governing their hearts by His word and Spirit;[40] and overcoming all their enemies by His almighty power and wisdom.[41] He does so in such manner and ways as are most consonant to His wonderful and unsearchable management; and all of free and absolute grace, without any condition foreseen in them to procure it.[42]

[38]John 6:37; 10:15-16; 17:9; Rom. 5:10. [39]John 17:6; Eph. 1:9; 1 John 5:20. [40]Rom. 8:9, 14. [41]Ps. 110:1; 1 Cor. 15:25-26. [42]John 3:8; Eph. 1:8.

9 This office of Mediator between God and man rightfully belongs only to Christ, who is the prophet, priest, and king of the church of God; and may not be either in whole, or any part thereof, transferred from Him to any other.[43]

[43]1 Tim. 2:5.

10 This number and order of offices is necessary; for in respect of our ignorance, we stand in need of His prophetic office;[44] and in respect of our alienation from God, and imperfection of the best of our services, we need His priestly office to reconcile us and present us acceptable unto God;[45] and in respect of our averseness and utter inability to return to God, and for our rescue and security from our spiritual adversaries, we need His kingly office to convince, subdue, draw, uphold, deliver, and preserve us to His heavenly kingdom.[46]

[44]John 1:18. [45]Col. 1:21; Gal. 5:17. [46]John 16:8; Ps. 110:3; Luke 1:74-75.

9. Free Will

1 God has furnished the will of man with that natural liberty and power of acting upon choice, that it is neither forced, nor by any necessity of nature determined to do good or evil.[1]

[1]Matt. 17:12; James 1:14; Deut. 30:19.

2 Man, in his state of innocency, had freedom and power to will and to do that which was good and well-pleasing to God,[2] but yet was unstable, so that he might fall from it.[3]

[2]Eccles. 7:29. [3]Gen. 3:6.

3 Man, by his fall into a state of sin, has wholly lost all ability of will to any spiritual good accompanying salvation.[4] So, as a natural man, being altogether averse from spiritual good, and dead in sin,[5] is not able by his own strength to convert himself, or to prepare himself for it.[6]

[4]Rom. 5:6; 8:7. [5]Eph. 2:1, 5. [6]Tit. 3:3-5; John 6:44.

4 When God converts a sinner, and translates him into the state of grace, He frees him from his natural bondage under sin[7] and by His grace alone enables him freely to will and to do that which is spiritually good.[8] However, due to his remaining corruptions, he does not carry out perfectly, nor only will, that which is good, but carries out and also wills that which is evil.[9]

[7]Col. 1:13; John 8:36. [8]Phil. 2:13. [9]Rom. 7:15, 18, 19, 21, 23.

5 This will of man is made perfectly and immutably free to do good alone in the state of glory only.[10]

[10]Eph. 4:13.

10. Effectual Calling

1 Those whom God has predestinated unto life, He is pleased in His appointed and accepted time, effectually to call,[1] by His word and Spirit, out of that state of sin and death in which they are by nature, to grace and salvation by Jesus Christ.[2] He enlightens their minds spiritually and savingly to understand the things of God;[3] takes away their heart of stone, and gives unto them a heart of flesh:[4] renews their wills, and by His almighty power enables them to do that which is good. He effectually draws them to Jesus Christ,[5] yet so as they come most freely, being made willing by His grace.[6]

[1]Rom. 8:30; 11:7; Eph. 1:10-11; 2 Thess. 2:13-14. [2]Eph. 2:1-6 [3]Acts 26:18; Eph. 1:17-18. [4]Ezek. 36:26. [5]Deut. 30:6; Ezek. 36:27; Eph. 1:19. [6]Ps. 110:3; Song 1:4.

2 This effectual call is of God's free and special grace alone, not from anything at all foreseen in man, nor from any power or agency in the creature,[7] being wholly passive in this matter, being dead in sins and trespasses, until being quickened and renewed by the Holy Spirit.[8] He is thereby enabled to answer this call, and to embrace the grace offered and conveyed in it, and that by no less power than that which raised up Christ from the dead.[9]

[7]2 Tim. 1:9; Eph. 2:8. [8]1 Cor. 2:14; Eph. 2:5; John 5:25. [9]Eph. 1:19-20.

3 Infants dying in infancy are regenerated and saved by Christ through the Spirit,[10] who works when, and where, and how He pleases.[11] So also are all elect persons, who are incapable of being outwardly called by the ministry of the word.

[10]John 3:3, 5-6. [11]John 3:8.

4 Others not elected, although they may be called by the ministry of the word, and may have some common operations of the Spirit,[12] yet not being effectually drawn by the Father, they neither will nor can truly come to Christ, and therefore cannot be saved.[13] Much less can men that receive not the Christian religion be saved, however diligently they live their lives according to the light of nature and the law of that religion they do profess.[14]

[12]Matt. 22:14; 13:20-21; Heb. 6:4-5. [13]John 6:44-45, 65;1 John 2:24-25. [14]Acts 4:12; John 4:22; 17:3.

11. Justification

1 Those whom God effectually calls, He also freely justifies,[1] not by infusing righteousness into them, but by pardoning their sins, and by accounting and accepting their persons as righteous.[2] They are justified not for anything wrought in them, or done by them, but for Christ's sake alone;[3] not by imputing faith itself, the act of believing, or any other obedience of the gospel to them, as their righteousness. They are justified by imputing Christ's active obedience to the whole law, and passive obedience in His death, for their whole and sole righteousness by faith.[4] This faith they have not of themselves; it is the gift of God.[5]

[1]Rom. 3:24; 8:30. [2]Rom. 4:5-8; Eph. 1:7. [3]1 Cor. 1:30-31; Rom. 5:17-19. [4]Phil. 3:8-9; Eph. 2:8-10. [5]John 1:12; Rom. 5:17.

2 The faith which thus receives and rests on Christ and His righteousness, is alone the instrument of justification.[6] Yet it is not alone in the person justified, but is ever accompanied with all other saving graces, and is no dead faith, but works by love.[7]

[6]Rom. 3:28. [7]Gal. 5:6; James 2:17, 22, 26.

3 Christ, by His obedience and death, did fully discharge the debt of all those that are justified; and did, by the sacrifice of Himself in the blood of His cross, undergoing in their stead the penalty due unto them, make a proper, real, and full satisfaction to God's justice in their behalf.[8] Yet, inasmuch as He was given by the Father for them, and His obedience and satisfaction accepted in their stead, and both freely, not for anything in them,[9] their justification is only of free grace, that both the exact justice and rich grace of God might be glorified in the justification of sinners.[10]

[8]Heb. 10:14; 1 Pet. 1:18-19; Isa. 53:5-6. [9]Rom. 8:32; 2 Cor. 5:21. [10]Rom. 3:26; Eph. 1:6-7; 2:7.

4 God did from all eternity decree to justify all the elect,[11] and Christ did in the fulness of time die for their sins, and rise again for their justification.[12] Nevertheless, they are not justified personally, until the Holy Spirit does in due time actually apply Christ unto them.[13]

[11]Gal. 3:8; 1 Pet. 1:2; 1 Tim. 2:6. [12]Rom. 4:25. [13]Col. 1:21-22; Tit. 3:4-7.

5 God does continue to forgive the sins of those that are justified,[14] and although they can never fall from the state of justification,[15] yet they may, by their sins, fall under God's fatherly displeasure.[16] In that condition they usually have not the light of His countenance restored unto them, until they humble themselves, confess their sins, beg pardon, and renew their faith and repentance.[17]

[14]Matt. 6:12; 1 John 1:7, 9. [15]John 10:28. [16]Ps. 89:31-33. [17]Ps. 32:5; Ps. 51; Matt. 26:75.

6 The justification of believers under the Old Testament was, in all these respects, one and the same with the justification of believers under the New Testament.[18]

[18]Gal. 3:9; Rom. 4:22-24.

12. Adoption

1 All those that are justified, God vouchsafed, in and for the sake of His only Son Jesus Christ, to make partakers of the grace of adoption,[1] by which they are taken into the number, and enjoy the liberties and privileges of children of God.[2] They have His name put upon them,[3] receive the spirit of adoption,[4] have access to the throne of grace with boldness, are enabled to cry Abba, Father,[5] are pitied,[6] protected,[7] provided for,[8] and chastened by Him as by a Father.[9] Yet, they are never cast off,[10] but sealed to the day of redemption,[11] and inherit the promises as heirs of everlasting salvation.[12]

[1]Eph. 1:5; Gal. 4:4-5. [2]John 1:12; Rom. 8:17. [3]2 Cor. 6:18; Rev. 3:12. [4]Rom. 8:15. [5]Gal. 4:6; Eph. 2:18. [6]Ps. 103:13. [7]Prov. 14:26. [8]1 Pet. 5:7. [9]Heb. 12:6. [10]Isa. 54:8-9; Lam. 3:31. [11]Eph. 4:30. [12]Heb. 1:14; 6:12.

13. Sanctification

1 They who are united to Christ, effectually called, and regenerated, having a new heart and a new spirit created in them through the virtue of Christ's death and resurrection, are also farther sanctified, really and personally,[1] through the same virtue, by His word and Spirit dwelling in them.[2] The dominion of the whole body of sin is destroyed,[3] and the several lusts from it are more and more weakened and mortified,[4] and they more and more made alive and strengthened in all saving graces,[5] to the practice of all true holiness, without which no man shall see the Lord.[6]

[1]Acts 20:32; Rom. 6:5-6. [2]John 17:17; Eph. 3:16-19; 1 Thess. 5:21-23. [3]Rom. 6:14. [4]Gal. 5:24. [5]Col. 1:11. [6]2 Cor. 7:1; Heb. 12:14.

2 This sanctification is throughout the whole man,[7] yet imperfect in this life. There abides still some remnants of corruption in every part,[8] from which arises a continual and irreconcilable war; the flesh lusting against the Spirit, and the Spirit against the flesh.[9]

[7]1 Thess. 5:23. [8]Rom. 7:18, 23. [9]Gal. 5:17; 1 Pet. 2:11.

3 In this war, although the remaining corruption for a time may much prevail,[10] yet, through the continual supply of strength from the sanctifying Spirit of Christ, the regenerate part does overcome.[11] So the saints grow in grace, perfecting holiness in the fear of God, pressing after a heavenly life, in gospel obedience to all the commands which Christ as head and king, in His word has prescribed for them.[12]

[10]Rom. 7:23. [11]Rom. 6:14. [12]Eph. 4:15-16; 2 Cor. 3:18; 7:1.

14. Saving Faith

1 The grace of faith, by which the elect are enabled to believe to the saving of their souls, is the work of the Spirit of Christ in their hearts,[1] and is ordinarily wrought by the ministry of the word.[2] By the ministry of the word also, and by the administration of baptism and the Lord's Supper, prayer, and other means appointed of God, that faith is increased and strengthened.[3]

[1]2 Cor. 4:13; Eph. 2:8. [2]Rom. 10:14, 17. [3]Luke 17:5; 1 Pet. 2:2; Acts 20:32.

2 By this faith a Christian believes to be true whatever is revealed in the word as by the authority of God Himself,[4] and also apprehends an excellency in it above all other writings and all things in the world,[5] as it bears forth the glory of God in His attributes, the excellency of Christ in His nature and offices, and the power and fulness of the Holy Spirit in His workings and operations. The Christian is enabled to cast his soul upon the truth thus believed;[6] and also acts differently upon that which each particular passage contains; yielding obedience to the commands,[7] trembling at the threats,[8] and embracing the promises of God for this life and that which is to come.[9] However, the principal acts of saving faith have immediate relation to Christ, accepting, receiving, and resting upon Him alone for justification, sanctification, and eternal life, by virtue of the covenant of grace.[10]

[4]Acts 24:14. [5]Ps. 19:7-10; 119:72. [6]2 Tim. 1:12. [7]John 15:14. [8]Isa. 66:2. [9]Heb. 11:13. [10]John 1:12; Acts 26:31; Gal. 2:20; Acts 15:11.

3 This faith, although it be different in degrees, and may be weak

or strong,[11] yet it is in the least degree of it different in the kind or nature of it, as is all other saving grace, from the faith and common grace of temporary believers.[12] Therefore, though it may be many times assailed and weakened, yet it gets the victory,[13] growing up in many to the attainment of a full assurance through Christ,[14] who is both the author and finisher of our faith.[15]

[11]Heb. 5:13-14; Matt. 6:30; Rom. 4:19-20. [12]2 Pet. 1:1. [13]Eph. 6:16; 1 John 5:4-5. [14]Heb. 6:11-12; Col. 2:2. [15]Heb. 12:2.

15. Repentance And Salvation

1 Those elect who are converted at riper years, having sometime lived in the state of nature, and in it served divers lusts and pleasures, God in their effectual calling gives them repentance unto life.[1]

[1]Tit. 3:2-5.

2 There is none that does good and sins not,[2] and the best of men may – through the power and deceitfulness of their corruption dwelling in them, with the prevalence of temptation – fall in to great sins and provocations. God has, in the covenant of grace, mercifully provided that believers so sinning and falling be renewed through repentance unto salvation.[3]

[2]Eccles. 7:20. [3]Luke 22:31-32.

3 This saving repentance is a gospel grace,[4] whereby a person, being by the Holy Spirit made sensible of the manifold evils of his sin, does, by faith in Christ, humble himself over it with godly sorrow, detestation of it, and self-abhorrence.[5] He prays for pardon and strength of grace, with a purpose and endeavour, by supplies of the Spirit's power, to walk before God and before in a way well-pleasing in all things.[6]

[4]Zech. 12:10; Acts 11:18. [5]Ezek.36:31; 2 Cor. 7:11. [6]Ps. 119:6, 128.

4 As repentance is to be continued through the whole course of our lives, upon the account of the body of death, and the inclinations

from it, so it is every man's duty to repent of his particular known sins particularly.[7]

[7]Luke 19:8; 1 Tim. 1:13, 15.

5 Such is the provision which God has made through Christ in the covenant of grace for the preservation of believers unto salvation, that although there is no sin so small as not to deserve damnation,[8] yet there is no sin so great that it shall bring damnation on them who repent,[9] which makes the constant preaching of repentance necessary.

[8]Rom. 6:23. [9]Isa. 1:16-18; 55:7.

16. Good Works

1 Good works are only such as God has commanded in His holy word,[1] and not such as without the warrant from it are devised by men out of blind zeal, or upon any claim to good intentions.[2]

[1]Mic. 6:8; Heb. 13:21. [2]Matt. 15:9; Isa. 29:13.

2 These good works, done in obedience to God's commandments, are the fruits and evidences of a true and lively faith.[3] By them believers manifest their thankfulness,[4] strengthen their assurance,[5] edify their brethren, adorn the profession of the gospel,[6] stop the mouths of the adversaries, and glorify God,[7] whose workmanship they are, created in Christ Jesus for that purpose,[8] so that with the fruit of their holiness, they may have the end eternal life.[9]

[3]James 2:18, 22. [4]Ps. 116:12-13. [5]1 John 2:3, 5; 2 Pet. 1:5-11. [6]Matt. 5:16. [7]1 Tim. 6:1; 1 Pet. 2:15; Phil. 1:11. [8]Eph. 2:10. [9]Rom. 6:22.

3 Their ability to do good works is not all of themselves, but wholly from the Spirit of Christ.[10] In order that they may be enabled to do so, besides the graces they have already received, it is necessary to have an actual influence of the same Holy Spirit, to work in them to will and to do of His good pleasure.[11] However, they are not as a result to grow negligent, as if they were not bound to perform any duty, unless upon a special motion of the Spirit, but they ought to be diligent in stirring up the grace of God that is in them.[12]

[10]John 15:4-5. [11]2 Cor. 3:5; Phil. 2:13. [12]Phil. 2:12; Heb. 6:11-12; Isa. 64:7.

4 They who in their obedience attain to the greatest height which is possible in this life, are so far from being able to earn merit for others, and to do more than God requires, such that they fall short of much which in duty they are bound to do.[13]

[13]Job 9:2-3; Gal. 5:17; Luke 17:10.

5 We cannot by our best works merit pardon of sin or eternal life at the hand of God, by reason of the great disproportion that is between our best works and the glory to come, and the infinite distance that is between us and God. By our best works we can neither profit nor satisfy God for the debt of sins we have committed.[14] When we have done all we can, we have done but our duty, and are unprofitable servants. As the works are good they proceed from His Spirit,[15] and as the works are wrought by us they are defiled and mixed with so much weakness and imperfection, that they cannot endure the severity of God's punishment.[16]

[14]Rom. 3:20, Eph. 2:8-9; Rom. 4:6. [15]Gal. 5:22-23. [16]Isa. 64:6; Ps. 143:2.

6 Yet despite the persons of believers being accepted through Christ, their good works also are accepted in Him;[17] not as though they were in this life wholly unblamable and unreprovable in God's sight, but that He, looking upon them in His Son, is pleased to accept and reward that which is sincere, although accompanied with many weaknesses and imperfections.[18]

[17]Eph. 1:6; 1 Pet. 2:5. [18]Matt. 25:21, 23; Heb. 6:10.

7 Works done by unregenerate men, may be in their essence things which God commands, and of good use both to themselves and others.[19] Yet because the works proceed not from a heart purified by faith,[20] nor are done in a right manner according to the word,[21] nor to a right end, namely the glory of God,[22] they are therefore sinful, and cannot please God, nor make a man fit to receive grace from God.[23] And yet their neglect of them is more sinful and displeasing to God.[24]

[19]2 Kings 10:30; 1 Kings 21:27, 29. [20]Gen. 4:5; Heb. 11:4, 6. [21]1 Cor. 13:1. [22]Matt. 6:2, 5. [23]Amos 5:21-22; Rom. 9:16; Tit. 3:5. [24]Job. 21:14-15; Matt. 24:41-43.

✳ ✳ ✳ ✳ ✳

17. The Perseverance
Of The Saints

1 Those whom God has accepted in the beloved, effectually called
and sanctified by His Spirit, and given the precious faith of His
elect, can neither totally nor finally fall from the state of grace, but
shall certainly persevere in it to the end, and be eternally saved.
This is because the gifts and callings of God are without repentance, from which He still begets and nourishes in them faith, repentance, love, joy, hope, and all the graces of the Spirit unto immortality.[1] Though many storms and floods arise and beat against
them, yet these things shall never be able to take them off that
foundation and rock which by faith they are fastened upon. Nevertheless, through unbelief and the temptations of Satan, the sensible sight of the light and love of God may for a time be clouded
and obscured from them.[2] Yet God is still the same, and they shall
be sure to be kept by the power of God unto salvation, where they
shall enjoy their purchased possession, for they are engraved upon
the palm of His hands, and their names have been written in the
book of life from all eternity.[3]

[1]John 10:28-29; Phil. 1:6; 2 Tim. 2:19; 1 John 2:19. [2]Ps. 89:31-
32; 1 Cor. 11:32. [3]Mal. 3:6.

2 This perseverance of the saints depends not upon their own free
will, but upon the immutability of the decree of election,[4] flowing
from the free and unchangeable love of God the Father, upon the
efficacy of the merit and intercession of Jesus Christ and union
with Him,[5] the oath of God,[6] the abiding of His Spirit, and the
seed of God within them,[7] and the nature of the covenant of

grace.[8] From all these arise also the certainty and infallibility of this perseverance.

[4]Rom. 8:30; 9:11, 16. [5]Rom. 5:9-10; John 14:19. [6]Heb. 6:17-18. [7]1 John 3:9. [8]Jer. 32:40.

3 The saints may, through the temptation of Satan and of the world, the prevalence of corruption remaining in them, and the neglect of means of their preservation, fall into grievous sins. They may for a time continue in sin,[9] whereby they incur God's displeasure and grieve His Holy Spirit,[10] cause their graces and comforts to be impaired,[11] have their hearts hardened, and their consciences wounded,[12] hurt and stumble others, and bring temporal judgments upon themselves.[13] Yet shall they renew their repentance and be preserved through faith in Christ Jesus to the end.[14]

[9]Matt. 26:70, 72, 74. [10]Isa. 64:5, 9; Eph. 4:30. [11]Ps. 51:10, 12. [12]Ps. 32:3-4. [13]2 Sam. 12:14. [14]Luke 22:32, 61-62.

18. Assurance Of Salvation

1 Although temporary believers, and other unregenerate men, may vainly deceive themselves with false hopes and carnal presumptions of being in the favour of God and state of salvation, such hope of theirs shall perish.[1] Yet such as truly believe in the Lord Jesus, and love Him in sincerity, endeavouring to walk in all good conscience before Him, may in this life be certainly assured that they are in the state of grace, and may rejoice in the hope of the glory of God.[2] This hope shall never make them disappointed.[3]

[1]Job 8:13-14; Matt. 7:22-23. [2]1 John 2:3; 3:14, 18-19, 21, 24; 5:13. [3]Rom. 5:2, 5.

2 This certainty is not a bare conjectural and probable persuasion grounded upon a fallible hope, but an infallible assurance of faith[4] founded on the blood and righteousness of Christ revealed in the gospel.[5] This certainty is grounded also upon the inward evidence of those graces of the Spirit unto which promises are made,[6] and on the testimony of the Spirit of adoption, witnessing with our spirits that we are the children of God.[7] A fruit from this is keeping the heart both humble and holy.[8]

[4]Heb. 6:11, 19. [5]Heb. 6:17-18. [6]2 Pet. 1:4-5, 10-11. [7]Rom. 8:15-16. [8]1 John 3:1-3.

3 This infallible assurance does not belong to the essence of faith, but a true believer may wait long, and struggle with many difficulties before he is partaker of it.[9] Yet being enabled by the Spirit to know the things which are freely given him from God, he may, without extraordinary revelation, with the right use of means, attain to assurance.[10] Therefore it is the duty of everyone to give

all diligence to make his calling and election sure, that thereby his heart may be enlarged in peace and joy in the Holy Spirit, in love and thankfulness to God, and in strength and cheerfulness for the duties of obedience. All these are the proper fruits of this assurance.[11] So far is it from inclining men to looseness.[12]

[9]Isa. 50:10; Ps. 88; Ps. 77:1-12. [10]1 John 4:13; Heb. 6:11-12. [11]Rom. 5:1, 2, 5; 14:17; Ps. 119:32. [12]Rom. 6:1-2; Tit. 2:11-12, 14.

4 True believers may have the assurance of their salvation in divers ways shaken, diminished, and suspended – as by negligence in preserving of it,[13] by falling into some special sin which wounds the conscience and grieves the Spirit[14] by some sudden or vehement temptation,[15] by God's withdrawing the light of His countenance – and allowing even such as fear Him to walk in darkness and to have no light.[16] Yet they are never left without the seed of God[17] and life of faith,[18] or love of Christ and the brethren, or sincerity of heart and conscience of duty – out of which, by the operation of the Spirit, this assurance may in due time be revived.[19] By these graces, in the meantime, they are preserved from utter despair.[20]

[13]Song 5:2, 3, 6. [14]Ps. 51:8, 12, 14. [15]Ps. 116:11; 77:7-8; 31:22. [16]Ps. 30:7. [17]1 John 3:9. [18]Luke 22:32. [19]Ps. 42:5, 11. [20]Lam. 3:26-31.

19. The Law Of God

1 God gave to Adam a law of complete obedience written in his heart, and a particular precept of not eating the fruit of the tree of knowledge of good and evil.[1] By this law he bound Adam and all his posterity to personal, entire, exact, and perpetual obedience,[2] promised life upon fulfilling it, and threatened death upon the breach of it, and endued him with power and ability to keep it.[3]

[1]Gen. 1:27; Eccles. 7:29. [2]Rom. 10:5. [3]Gal. 3:10, 12.

2 The same law that was first written in the heart of man continued to be a perfect rule of righteousness after the fall,[4] and was delivered by God upon Mount Sinai, in ten commandments, and written in two tables, the four first containing our duty towards God, and the other six, our duty to man.[5]

[4]Rom. 2:14-15. [5]Deut. 10:4.

3 Besides this law, commonly called moral, God was pleased to give to the people of Israel ceremonial laws. These ceremonial laws contain several typological ordinances, partly of worship, which prefigured Christ, His graces, actions, sufferings, and benefits,[6] and partly holding forth divers instructions of moral duties.[7] All these ceremonial laws were appointed until the time of fulfilment by Jesus Christ the true Messiah and only law-giver, who was furnished with power from the Father to end and take them away.[8]

[6]Heb. 10:1; Col. 2:17. [7]1 Cor. 5:7 [8]Col. 2:14, 16-17; Eph. 2:14, 16.

4 To them also He gave sundry judicial laws, which expired together with the civil state of that people, not obliging any now by virtue

of that institution. Only their principles of equity are for modern use.[9]

[9]1 Cor. 9:8-10.

5 The moral law does for ever bind all, justified persons as well as others, to the obedience of it,[10] not only in regard to the matter contained in it, but also in respect of the authority of God the Creator, who gave it.[11] Neither does Christ in the gospel in any way dissolve, but much strengthen, this obligation.[12]

[10]Rom.13:8-10; James 2:8, 10-12. [11]James 2:10-11. [12]Matt. 5:17-19; Rom. 3:31.

6 Although true believers are not under the law as a covenant of works, to be justified or condemned by it,[13] yet it is of great use to them as well as to others, in that as a rule of life, it informs them of the will of God and their duty, and directs and binds them to walk accordingly.

The law also reveals the sinful pollutions of their natures, hearts, and lives, so that by examining themselves, they may come to further conviction of, humiliation for, and hatred against, sin.[14] They will also gain a clearer sight of the need they have of Christ and the perfection of His obedience.

The law is likewise of use to the regenerate to restrain their corruptions, in that it forbids sin. The threatenings of the law serve to show what even their sins deserve, and what afflictions in this life they may expect for them, although freed from the curse and undiminished demand of the law.

These promises of the law likewise show them God's approval of obedience, and what blessings they may expect upon the performance of it, though not because they have kept the law as a covenant of works. If a man does good and refrains from evil, because the law encourages to the good and deters from the evil, it is no evidence that he is under the law and not under grace.[15]

[13]Rom. 6:14; Gal. 2:16; Rom. 8:1; 10:4. [14]Rom. 3:20; 7:7, etc. [15]Rom. 6:12-14. 1 Pet. 3:8-13.

7 The aforementioned uses of the law are not contrary to the grace of the gospel, but do sweetly comply with it,[16] as the Spirit of

Christ subdues and enables the will of man to do freely and cheerfully what the will of God, as revealed in the law, requires to be done.[17]

[16]Gal. 3:21. [17]Ezek. 36:27.

20. The Gospel And Its Gracious Extent

1 The covenant of works being broken by sin, and made unprofitable for life, God was pleased to give forth the promise of Christ, the seed of the woman, as the means of calling the elect, and begetting in them faith and repentance.[1] In this promise the gospel, as to the substance of it, was revealed, and made effectual for the conversion and salvation of sinners.[2]

[1]Gen. 3:15. [2]Rev. 13:8.

2 This promise of Christ, and salvation by Him, is revealed only by the word of God.[3] Neither the works of creation or providence, nor the light of nature, make known Christ, or the grace by Him, even in a general or obscure way.[4] Much less men devoid of the revelation of Him by the promise or gospel, are able through these to attain saving faith or repentance.[5]

[3]Rom. 1:17. [4]Rom. 10:14-15, 17. [5]Prov. 29:18; Isa. 25:7; 60:2-3.

3 The revelation of the gospel to sinners, made in various times and diverse places, together with the promises and precepts which belong to gospel obedience, to the nations and persons to whom it is granted, is merely of the sovereign will and good pleasure of God.[6] This revelation of the gospel is not given by virtue of any foreseen good done by men's natural abilities, or by human wisdom, which none ever did, or can do.[7] Therefore in all ages, the preaching of the gospel has been granted unto persons and nations, to greater or smaller extent, in various degrees, according to the counsel of the will of God.

[6]Ps. 147:20; Acts 16:7. [7]Rom. 1:18-32.

4 The gospel is the only outward means of revealing Christ and saving grace, and is, as such, abundantly sufficient for that. Yet, in order that men who are dead in trespasses may be born again, made alive or regenerated, there is necessary an effectual invincible work of the Holy Spirit upon the whole soul, to produce in them a new spiritual life.[8] Without this, no other means will effect their conversion to God.[9]

[8]Ps. 110:3; 1 Cor. 2:14; Eph. 1:19-20. [9]John 6:44; 2 Cor. 4:4, 6.

21. Liberty And Conscience

1 The liberty which Christ has purchased for believers under the gospel consists, firstly, in their freedom from the guilt of sin, the condemning wrath of God, the rigour and curse of the law.[1]

Secondly, it consists in their being delivered from this present evil world,[2] bondage to Satan,[3] and dominion of sin,[4] from the evil of afflictions,[5] the fear and sting of death, the victory of the grave,[6] and everlasting damnation.[7]

Thirdly, it consists in their free access to God, and their yielding obedience unto Him, not out of slavish fear,[8] but a childlike love and willing mind.[9]

All these were experienced also by believers under the law for the substance of them;[10] but under the New Testament the liberty of Christians is further enlarged, – (i) in their freedom from the yoke of a ceremonial law, to which the Jewish church was subjected, and (ii) in greater boldness of access to the throne of grace, and (iii) in fuller communications of the free Spirit of God, than normally experienced by believers under the law.[11]

[1]Gal. 3:13. [2]Gal. 1:4. [3]Acts 26:18. [4]Rom. 8:3. [5]Rom. 8:28. [6]1 Cor. 15:54-57. [7]2 Thess. 1:10. [8]Rom. 8:15. [9]Luke 1:73-75; 1 John 4:18. [10]Gal. 3:9, 14. [11]John 7:38-39; Heb. 10:19-21.

2 God alone is Lord of the conscience,[12] and has left it free from the doctrines and commandments of men which are in any thing contrary to His word, or not contained in it.[13] So that to believe such doctrines, or obey such commands against conscience, it so betray true liberty of conscience.[14] To require an implicit faith, an

absolute and blind obedience, is to destroy liberty of conscience and reason also.[15]

[12]James 4:12; Rom. 14:4. [13]Acts 4:19, 29; 1 Cor. 7:23; Matt. 15:9. [14]Col. 2:20, 22-23. [15]1 Cor. 3:5; 2 Cor. 1:24.

3 They who misuse Christian liberty by practising any sin, or cherishing any sinful lust, pervert the main purpose of the grace of the gospel to their own destruction.[16] They completely destroy the purpose of Christian liberty, which is, that being delivered out of the hands of all our enemies, we might serve the Lord without fear, in holiness and righteousness before Him, all the days of our lives.[17]

[16]Rom. 6:1-2. [17]Gal. 5:13; 2 Pet. 2:18, 21.

22. Worship And The Sabbath

1 The light of nature shows that there is a God, who has lordship and sovereignty over all, is just, good and does good to all. Therefore God is to be feared, loved, praised, called upon, trusted in, and served, with all the heart and all the soul, and with all the might.[1] But the acceptable way of worshipping the true God, is instituted by Himself,[2] and so limited by His own revealed will, that He may not be worshipped according to the imagination and devices of men, nor the suggestions of Satan, under any visible representations, or any other way not prescribed in the Holy Scriptures.[3]

[1]Jer. 10:7; Mark 12:33. [2]Deut. 12:32. [3]Exod. 20:4-6.

2 Worship is to be given to God the Father, Son, and Holy Spirit, and to Him alone;[4] not to angels, saints, or any other creatures.[5] Since the fall, worship is not to be given without a mediator,[6] nor by the mediation of any other but Christ alone.[7]

[4]Matt. 4:9-10; John 4:23; Matt. 28:19. [5]Rom. 1:25; Col. 2:18; Rev. 19:10. [6]John 14:6. [7]1 Tim. 2:5.

3 Prayer, with thanksgiving, being one part of natural worship, is by God required of all men.[8] But that it may be accepted, it is to be made in the name of the Son,[9] by the help of the Spirit,[10] according to His will;[11] with understanding, reverence, humility, fervency, faith, love, and perseverance; and when with others, in a known tongue.[12]

121

[8]Ps. 95:1-7; 65:2. [9]John 14:13-14. [10]Rom. 8:26. [11]1 John 5:14.
[12]1 Cor. 14:16-17.

4 Prayer is to be made for things lawful, and for all sorts of men living, or that shall live in the future;[13] but not for the dead,[14] nor for those known to have sinned the sin leading to death.[15]

[13]1 Tim. 2:1-2; 2 Sam. 7:29. [14]2 Sam. 12:21-23. [15]1 John 5:16.

5 The reading of the Scriptures,[16] preaching, and hearing the word of God,[17] teaching and admonishing one another in psalms, hymns, and spiritual songs, singing with grace in our hearts to the Lord,[18] as also the administration of baptism,[19] and the Lord's Supper,[20] are all parts of the worship of God. These are to be performed in obedience to Him, with understanding, faith, reverence, and godly fear. Moreover, solemn humiliation, with fastings,[21] and thanksgivings, upon special occasions, ought to be used in a holy and reverent manner.[22]

[16]1 Tim. 4:13. [17]2 Tim. 4:2; Luke 8:18. [18]Col. 3:16; Eph. 5:19.
[19]Matt. 28:19-20. [20]1 Cor. 11:26. [21]Esther 4:16; Joel 2:12.
[22]Exod. 15:1-19; Ps. 107.

6 Neither prayer nor any other part of worship, which is now under the gospel, tied to, or made more acceptable by any place in which it is performed, or towards which it is directed. Instead, God is to be worshipped everywhere in spirit and in truth,[23] whether in private families[24] daily,[25] and in secret each individually,[26] and especially solemnly in the public assemblies. These are not to be carelessly nor wilfully neglected or forsaken, when God by His word or providence calls to do them.[27]

[23]John 4:21; Mal. 1:11; 1 Tim. 2:8. [24]Acts 10:2. [25]Matt. 6:11;
Ps. 55:17. [26]Matt. 6:6. [27]Heb. 10:25; Acts 2:42.

7 It is the law of nature, that in general a proportion of time, by God's appointment, should be set apart for the worship of God. By His word, in a positive moral, and perpetual commandment, binding all men, in all ages, He has particularly appointed one day in seven for a Sabbath to be kept holy unto Him.[28] From the beginning of the world to the resurrection of Christ, the Sabbath was the last day of the week, and from the resurrection of Christ

it was changed to the first day of the week, which is called the Lord's Day.[29] This is to be continued to the end of the world as the Christian Sabbath, the observation of the last day of the week being abolished.

[28]Exod. 20:8. [29]1 Cor. 16:1-2; Acts 20:7; Rev. 1:10.

8 The Sabbath is kept holy unto the Lord when men, after a due preparing of their hearts and ordering their common affairs beforehand, not only observe a holy rest all day – from their own works, words and thoughts, as well as their worldly employment and recreations[30] – but are occupied throughout that day in the public and private acts of worship, and in the duties of necessity and mercy.[31]

[30]Isa. 58:13; Neh. 13:15-22. [31]Matt. 12:1-13.

23. Lawful Oaths And Vows

1 A lawful oath is a part of religious worship, in which the person swearing in truth, righteousness, and understanding, solemnly calls God to witness what he swears,[1] and to judge him according to the truth or falseness of it.[2]

[1]Exod. 20:7; Deut. 10:20; Jer. 4:2. [2]2 Chron. 6:22-23.

2 Only in the name of God men ought to swear; and it is to be carried out with all holy fear and reverence. Therefore to swear vainly or rashly by that glorious and dreadful name, or to swear at all by any other thing, is sinful, and to be abhorred.[3] Yet in matters of importance and seriousness, for confirmation of truth, and ending all strife, an oath is warranted by the word of God.[4] Therefore a lawful oath imposed by lawful authority in such matters, ought to be taken.[5]

[3]Matt. 5:34, 37; James 5:12. [4]Heb. 6:16; 2 Cor. 1:23. [5]Neh. 13:25.

3 Whoever takes an oath warranted by the word of God, ought duly to consider the weightiness of so solemn an act, and affirm nothing but what he knows to be truth; for by rash, false, and vain oaths, the Lord is provoked, and because of them the land suffers.[6]

[6]Lev. 19:12; Jer. 23:10.

4 An oath is to be taken in the plain and common meaning of the words, without equivocation or mental reservation.[7]

[7]Ps. 24:4.

5 A vow, which is not to be made to any creature, but to God alone, is to be made and performed with all utmost care and faithfulness.[8] But Roman Catholic monastical vows of perpetual single life,[9] professed poverty,[10] and unquestioning obedience to the church, are so far from being degrees of higher perfection, that they are superstitious and sinful snares. No Christian may entangle himself in these.[11]

[8]Ps. 76:11; Gen. 28:20-22. [9]1 Cor. 7:2, 9. [10]Eph. 4:28. [11]Matt. 19:11.

24. The Civil Magistrate

1 God, the supreme Lord and King of all the world, has ordained civil magistrates to be under Him, over the people, for His own glory and the public good. To this end He has armed them with the power of the sword, for defence and encouragement of them that do good, and for the punishment of evil doers.[1]

[1]Rom. 13:1-4.

2 It is lawful for Christians to accept and execute the office of a magistrate when called to it. In the execution of that office, they ought especially to maintain justice and peace,[2] according to the wholesome laws of each nation. For that end they may lawfully, under the New Testament, wage war upon just and necessary occasions.[3]

[2]2 Sam. 23:3, Ps. 82:3-4. [3]Luke 3:14.

3 Because civil magistrates are set up by God for the ends mentioned before, subjection by us in the Lord – in all lawful things commanded by them – ought to be given, not only to avoid punishment, but for conscience's sake.[4] And we ought to make supplications and prayers for kings and all that are in authority, that under them we may live a quiet and peaceable life, in all godliness and honesty.[5]

[4]Rom. 8:5-7; 1 Pet. 2:17. [5]1 Tim. 2:1-2.

25. Marriage

1 Marriage is to be between one man and one woman. It is not lawful for any man to have more than one wife, nor for any woman to have more than one husband at the same time.[1]

[1]Gen. 2:24; Mal. 2:15; Matt. 19:5-6.

2 Marriage was ordained for the mutual help of husband and wife,[2] for the increase of mankind in a legitimate way,[3] and for preventing immorality.[4]

[2]Gen. 2:18. [3]Gen. 1:28. [4]1 Cor. 7:2, 9.

3 It is lawful for all sorts of people to marry, who are able with judgment to give their consent.[5] Yet it is the duty of Christians to marry in the Lord.[6] Therefore such as profess the true religion, should not marry with infidels, or idolators. Neither should those who are godly, be unequally yoked, by marrying with those who are wicked in their life, or maintain damnable heresy.[7]

[5]Heb. 13:4; 1 Tim. 4:3. [6]1 Cor. 7:39. [7]Neh. 13:25-27.

26. The Church

1 The catholic or universal church, which (with respect to the internal work of the Spirit and truth of grace) may be called invisible, consists of the whole number of the elect, that have been, are, or shall be gathered into one, under Christ, who is the Head. This church is the wife, the body, the fulness of Him that fills all in all.[1]

[1]Heb. 12:23; Col. 1:18; Eph. 1:10, 22-23; 5:23, 27, 32.

2 All persons throughout the world, professing the faith of the gospel, and obedience to God by Christ according to that gospel, and do not destroy their own profession by any errors that attack the foundation, or by unholiness of behaviour, are and may be called visible saints.[2] Of such persons ought all particular congregations to be constituted.[3]

[2]1 Cor. 1:2; Acts 11:26. [3]Rom. 1:7; Eph. 1:20-22.

3 The purest churches under heaven are disposed to mixture and error.[4] Some have so degenerated as to become no churches of Christ, but synagogues of Satan.[5] Nevertheless Christ always has had, and ever shall have a kingdom in this world, to the end of time, of such as believe in Him, and make profession of His name.[6]

[4]1 Cor. 5; Rev. 2 & 3. [5]Rev. 18:2; 2 Thess. 2:11-12. [6]Matt. 16:18; Ps. 72:17; 102:28; Rev. 12:17.

4 The Lord Jesus Christ is the head of the church, in whom, by the appointment of the Father, all power for the calling, institution, order, or government of the church, is invested in a supreme and sovereign manner.[7] The Pope of Rome cannot in any sense be head of the church, but is that antichrist, that man of sin, and

son of perdition, who exalts himself in the church against Christ, and all that is called God, whom the Lord shall destroy with the brightness of His coming.[8]

[7]Col. 1:18; Matt. 28:18-20; Eph. 4:11-12. [8]2 Thess. 2:2-9.

5 In the execution of this power with which He is so entrusted, the Lord Jesus calls out of the world to Himself, through the ministry of His word, by His Spirit, those that are given to Him by His Father,[9] that they may walk before Him in all the ways of obedience, which He prescribes to them in His word.[10] Those thus called, He commands to walk together in particular societies, or churches, for their mutual edification, and the due performance of that public worship, which He requires of them in the world.[11]

[9]John 10:16; John 12:32. [10]Matt. 28:20. [11]Matt. 18:15-20.

6 The members of these churches are saints by calling, visibly manifesting and evidencing (in and by their profession and walking) their obedience to that call of Christ.[12] They willingly consent to walk together, according to the teaching of Christ – giving up themselves to the Lord, and one to another, by the will of God, in professed subjection to the ordinances of the gospel.[13]

[12]Rom. 1:7; 1 Cor. 1:2. [13]Acts 2:41-42; 5:13-14; 2 Cor. 9:13.

7 To each of these churches thus gathered, according to His mind declared in His word, He has given all the power and authority, which is in any way needful for their carrying on the manner of worship and discipline, which He has instituted for them to observe. He has also given commands and rules for the due and right execution of that power.[14]

[14]Matt. 18:17-18; 1 Cor. 5:4-5, 13; 2 Cor. 2:6-8.

8 A particular church, gathered and completely organised according to the mind of Christ, consists of officers and members. The officers appointed by Christ to be chosen and set apart by the church (so called and gathered), for the special administration of ordinances, and execution of power or duty, which He entrusts them with, or calls them to, are bishops or elders, and deacons.[15] This pattern of church order is to be continued to the end of the world.

[15]Acts 20:17, 28; Phil. 1:1.

9 The way appointed by Christ for the calling of any person, fitted and gifted by the Holy Spirit, for the office of bishop or elder in a church, is, that he be chosen by the voting of the church itself.[16] He should be solemnly set apart by fasting and prayer, with laying on of hands of the eldership of the church, if there be any before constituted.[17] A deacon is to be chosen by the similar voting, and set apart by prayer, and the similar laying on of hands.[18]

[16]Acts 14:23. [17]1 Tim. 4:14. [18]Acts 6:3, 5-6.

10 The work of pastors being constantly to handle the service of Christ, in His churches, in the ministry of the word and prayer, with watching for their souls, as those that must give an account to Him.[19] It is incumbent on the churches they minister to, not only to give them all due respect, but also to communicate to them of all their good things, according to their ability.[20] This must be done so that they may have a comfortable supply, without being themselves entangled in secular affairs,[21] and be capable of exercising hospitality towards others.[22] This is required by the law of nature, and by the express order of our Lord Jesus, who has ordained that those who preach the gospel should live from the gospel.[23]

[19]Acts 6:4; Heb. 13:17. [20]1 Tim. 5:17-18; Gal. 6:6-7. [21]2 Tim. 2:4. [22]1 Tim. 3:2. [23]1 Cor. 9:6-14.

11 Although it be incumbent on the bishops or pastors of the churches, to be urgent in preaching the word, by way of office, yet the work of preaching the word is not so exclusively confined to them but others also who are gifted and fitted by the Holy Spirit for it, and approved and called by the church, may and ought to perform it.[24]

[24]Acts 11:19-21; 1 Pet. 4:10-11.

12 All believers are bound to join themselves to particular churches, when and where they have opportunity so to do. All who are admitted into the privileges of a church, are also under the discipline and government of that church, in accordance to the rule of Christ.[25]

[25]1 Thess. 5:14; 2 Thess. 3:6, 14-15.

13 No church members, because of any offence made against them, having performed their duty required of them towards the person who caused the offence, ought to disturb any church order, or absent themselves from the meetings of the church, or administration of any ordinances, on account of such offence caused by their fellow members. They are to wait upon Christ, in the further action of the church.[26]

[26]Matt. 18:15-17; Eph. 4:2-3.

14 Each church, and all the members of it, are obligated to pray continually for the good and prosperity of all the churches of Christ,[27] in all places, and upon all occasions to further everyone within the bounds of their places and callings, in the exercise of their gifts and graces. The churches, when planted by the providence of God, ought to hold communion among themselves, for their peace, increase of love, and mutual edification, so as to enjoy the opportunity and benefit of such communion.[28]

[27]Eph. 6:18; Ps. 122:6. [28]Rom. 16:1-2; 3 John 8-10.

15 In cases of difficulties or differences, either in point of doctrine or administration, in which either the churches in general are concerned, or any one church, in their peace, union, and edification, or any member or members of any church are injured, in or by any disciplinary proceedings not agreeable to truth and order, it is in accordance to the mind of Christ, that many churches holding communion together, do, through their messengers, meet to consider, and give their advice about that matter in dispute, and to report to all the churches concerned.[29] However, these messengers assembled, are not entrusted with any church power properly so called, or with any jurisdiction over the churches themselves, to exercise any censures either over any churches or persons, or to impose their determination on the churches or officers.[30]

[29]Acts 15:2, 4, 6, 22, 23, 25. [30]2 Cor. 1:24; 1 John 4:1.

27. The Communion Of Saints

1 All saints that are united to Jesus Christ, their head, by His Spirit, and faith, although they are not made thereby one person with Him, have fellowship in His graces, sufferings, death, resurrection, and glory.[1] Being united to one another in love, they have communion in each other's gifts and graces.[2] They are obliged to the performance of such duties, public and private, in an orderly way, as helpful to their mutual good, both spiritually and physically.[3]

[1] 1 John 1:3; John 1:16; Phil. 3:10; Rom. 6:5-6. [2] Eph. 4:15-16; 1 Cor. 12:7; 3:21-23. [3] 1 Thess. 5:11, 14; Rom. 1:12; 1 John 3:17-18; Gal. 6:10.

2 Saints by profession are bound to maintain a holy fellowship and communion in the worship of God, and in performing such other spiritual services as tend to their mutual edification.[4] They are also to relieve each other in outward things according to their different abilities, and needs.[5] This communion, according to the rule of the gospel, applies especially in the relation in which they stand – whether in families,[6] or churches.[7] However, as God offers opportunity, this communion is to be extended to all the household of faith, who in every place call upon the name of the Lord Jesus. Nevertheless their communion one with another as saints, does not take away or infringe the right or ownership of each man in his goods and possessions.[8]

135

[4]Heb. 10:24-25; 3:12-13. [5]Acts 11:29-30. [6]Eph. 6:4. [7]1 Cor. 12:14-27. [1]Acts 5:4; Eph. 4:28.

✳ ✳ ✳ ✳ ✳

28. Baptism And The Lord's Supper

1 Baptism and the Lord's Supper are ordinances of positive and sovereign institution, appointed by the Lord Jesus, the only law-giver, to be continued in His church to the end of the world.[1]

[1]Matt. 28:19-20; 1 Cor. 11:26.

2 These holy appointments are to be administered by those only who are qualified and called to it, according to the commission of Christ.[2]

[2]Matt. 28:19; 1 Cor. 4:1.

29. Baptism

1 Baptism is an ordinance of the New Testament, ordained by Jesus Christ, to be to the party baptised, a sign of his fellowship with Him, in His death and resurrection; of his being engrafted into Him;[1] of remission of sins;[2] and of his giving up unto God, through Jesus Christ, to live and walk in newness of life.[3]

[1]Rom. 6:3-5; Col. 2:12; Gal. 3:27.   [2]Mark 1:4; Acts 22:16. [3]Rom. 6:4.

2 Those who do actually profess repentance towards God, faith in, and obedience to, our Lord Jesus Christ, are the only proper subjects of this ordinance.[4]

[4]Mark 16:16; Acts 8:36-37; 2:41; 8:12; 18:8.

3 The outward element to be used in this ordinance is water, in which the party is to be baptised in the name of the Father, and of the Son, and of the Holy Spirit.[5]

[5]Matt. 28:19-20; Acts 8:38.

4 Immersion, or dipping of the person in water, is necessary to the due administration of this ordinance.[6]

[6]Matt. 3:16; John 3:23.

30. The Lord's Supper

1 The supper of the Lord Jesus was instituted by Him the same night in which He was betrayed, to be observed in His churches, to the end of the world for the perpetual remembrance, and showing forth the sacrifice of Himself in His death.[1] It is also to confirm the faith of believers in all the benefits of His death, including: (i) their spiritual nourishment, and growth in Him; (ii) their further engagement in, and to all duties which they owe to Him; and (iii) to be a bond and pledge of their communion with Him, and with each other.[2]

[1]1 Cor. 11:23-26. [2]1 Cor. 10:16-17, 21.

2 In this ordinance Christ is not offered up to His Father, nor any real sacrifice made at all for remission of sin of the living or dead, but only a memorial of that one offering up of Himself by Himself upon the cross, once for all,[3] with a spiritual offering of all possible praise unto God for His sacrificial death.[4] Therefore the Roman Catholic sacrifice of the mass, as they call it, is most abominable, injurious to Christ's own sacrifice, the only propitiation for all the sins of the elect.

[3]Heb. 9:25-26, 28. [4]1 Cor. 11:24; Matt. 26:26-27.

3 The Lord Jesus has, in this ordinance, appointed His ministers to pray and bless the elements of bread and wine – and so setting them apart from a common to a holy use – and to take and break the bread, then to take the cup, and they partaking also themselves, to give both to the partakers.[5]

[5]1 Cor. 11:23-26, etc.

4 The denial of the cup to the people, worshipping the elements, the lifting them up, or carrying them about for adoration, and reserving them for any false religious use, are all contrary to the nature of this ordinance, and to the institution of Christ.[6]

[6]Matt. 26:26-28; 15:9; Exod. 20:4-5.

5 The outward elements in this ordinance, duly set apart to the use ordained by Christ, have such relation to Him crucified, as that truly, although in terms used figuratively, they are sometimes called by the names of the things they represent, namely, the body and blood of Christ.[7] However, in substance and nature, they still remain truly and only bread and wine, as they were before.[8]

[7]1 Cor. 11:27. [8]1 Cor. 11:26-28.

6 That doctrine which maintains a change of the substance of bread and wine, into the substance of Christ's body and blood, commonly called transubstantiation, by consecration of a priest, or by any other way, is repugnant not only to Scripture,[9] but even to common sense and reason, overthrows the nature of the ordinance, and has been, and is, the cause of many superstitions and gross idolatries.[10]

[9]Acts 3:21; Luke 24:6, 39. [10]1 Cor. 11:24-25.

7 Worthy receivers, outwardly partaking of the visible elements in this ordinance, do also inwardly by faith, really and indeed – yet not physically and materially, but spiritually – receive, and feed upon Christ crucified, and all the benefits of His death. The body and blood of Christ is not materially or physically, but spiritually, present to the faith of believers in that ordinance, as the elements themselves are to their outward senses.[11]

[11]1 Cor. 10:16; 11:23-26.

8 All ignorant and ungodly persons, as they are unfit to enjoy communion with Christ, so are they unworthy of the Lord's table, and cannot, without great sin against him, while they remain such,

partake of these holy mysteries, or be admitted to the table.[12] Indeed, those who receive unworthily, are guilty of the body and blood of the Lord, eating and drinking judgment to themselves.[13]

[12] 2 Cor. 6:14-15. [13] 1 Cor. 11:29; Matt. 7:6.

31. Death And
The Resurrection

1 The bodies of men after death return to dust, and undergo corruption,[1] but their souls, which neither die nor sleep, having an immortal subsistence, immediately return to God who gave them.[2] The souls of the righteous are then made perfect in holiness, and received into Paradise, where they are with Christ, and behold the face of God in light and glory, waiting for the full redemption of their bodies.[3] The souls of the wicked are cast into hell, where they remain in torment and under darkness, reserved to the judgment of the great day.[4] Besides these two places, for souls separated from their bodies, the Scripture acknowledges none.

[1]Gen. 3:19; Acts 13:36. [2]Eccles. 12:7. [3]Luke 23:43; 2 Cor. 5:1, 6, 8; Phil. 1:23; Heb. 12:23. [4]Jude 6, 7; 1 Peter 3:19; Luke 16:23-24.

2 On the last day, such of the saints as are still alive, shall not sleep, but be changed.[5] All the dead shall be raised up with the selfsame bodies, and none other,[6] although with different qualities, which shall be united again to their souls for ever.[7]

[5]1 Cor. 15:51-52; 1 Thess. 4:17. [6]Job 19:26-27. [7]1 Cor. 15:42-43.

3 The bodies of the unjust shall, by the power of Christ, be raised to dishonour. The bodies of the just shall, by His Spirit, be raised to honour, and be made conformable to His own glorious body.[8]

[8]Acts 24:15; John 5:28-29; Phil. 3:21.

32. The Last Judgement

1 God has appointed a day in which He will judge the world in righteousness, by Jesus Christ,[1] to whom all power and judgment is given from the Father. On that day, not only the apostate angels shall be judged,[1] but likewise all persons that have lived upon the earth shall appear before the tribunal of Christ. They shall give an account of their thoughts, words, and deeds, and receive according to what they have done in the body, whether good or evil.[3]

[1]Acts 17:31; John 5:22, 27. [2]1 Cor. 6:3; Jude 6. [3]2 Cor. 5:10; Eccles. 12:14; Matt. 12:36; Rom. 14:10, 12; Matt. 25:32-46.

2 The end of appointing this day by God is for the manifestation of the glory of His mercy in the eternal salvation of the elect, and of His justice in the eternal damnation of the reprobate, who are wicked and disobedient.[4] Then the righteous shall go into everlasting life, and receive that fulness of joy and glory with everlasting rewards, in the presence of the Lord. The wicked who know not God, and obey not the gospel of Jesus Christ, shall be cast aside into everlasting torments,[5] and punished with everlasting destruction, from the presence of the Lord, and from the glory of His power.[6]

[4]Rom. 9:22-23. [5]Matt. 25:21, 34; 2 Tim. 4:8. [6]Matt. 25:46; Mark 9:48; 2 Thess. 1:7-10.

3 Christ wants us to be certainly persuaded that there shall be a day of judgment, both to deter all men from sin,[7] and for the greater consolation of the godly in their adversity.[8] He has kept the day unknown to men, so that they may shake off all carnal security,

147

and be always watchful, because they know not at what hour the Lord will come,[9] and may ever be prepared to say, "Come Lord Jesus, come quickly."[10] Amen.

[7]2 Cor. 5:10-11. [8]2 Thess. 1:5-7. [9]Mark 13:35-37; Luke 12:35-40. [10]Rev. 22:20

Other books by the same author:

Made in the USA
Middletown, DE
25 February 2022

61804589R00089